AN EXCERPT FROM
THE BOOK OF

HEBREWS

(CHAPTER 11:1-40)

THE
PREACHER'S
OUTLINE & SERMON
BIBLE®

NEW TESTAMENT

KING JAMES VERSION

Leadership Ministries Worldwide
Chattanooga, TN

The Preacher's Outline & Sermon Bible® is written for God's people to use in their preparation for preaching and teaching. Leadership Ministries Worldwide wants God's people to use *The Preacher's Outline & Sermon Bible*®. The purpose of the copyright is to prevent the reproduction, misuse, and abuse of the material.

May our Lord bless us all as we preach, teach, and write for Him, fulfilling His great commission to make disciples of all nations.

Please address all requests for information or permission to:
Leadership Ministries Worldwide
1928 Central Avenue
Chattanooga, TN 37408
Ph.# (423) 855-2181   FAX (423) 855-8616   E-Mail info@lmw.org
http://www.lmw.org

Library of Congress Catalog Card Number: 96-75921
International Standard Book Number: 978-1-57407-140-5

Printed in the United States of America

LEADERSHIP MINISTRIES WORLDWIDE

DEDICATED

To all the men and women of the world
who preach and teach the Gospel of
our Lord Jesus Christ and
to the Mercy and Grace of God

- Demonstrated to us in Christ Jesus our Lord.

  In him we have redemption through his blood, the forgiveness of sins, in accordance with the riches of God's grace. (Ep.1:7)

- Out of the mercy and grace of God, His Word has flowed. Let every person know that God will have mercy upon him, forgiving and using him to fulfill His glorious plan of salvation.

  For God so loved the world that he gave his one and only Son, that whoever believes in him shall not perish but have eternal life. For God did not send his Son into the world to condemn the world, but to save the world through him. (Jn.3:16-17)

  This is good, and pleases God our Savior, who wants all men to be saved and to come to a knowledge of the truth. (1 Ti.2:3-4)

6/10

The Preacher's Outline & Sermon Bible®

is written for God's servants to use in their study, teaching, and preaching of God's Holy Word...

- to share the Word of God with the world.
- to help believers, both ministers and laypersons, in their understanding, preaching, and teaching of God's Word.
- to do everything we possibly can to lead men, women, boys, and girls to give their hearts and lives to Jesus Christ and to secure the eternal life that He offers.
- to do all we can to minister to the needy of the world.
- to give Jesus Christ His proper place, the place the Word gives Him. Therefore, no work of Leadership Ministries Worldwide—no Outline Bible Resources—will ever be personalized.

ACKNOWLEDGMENTS AND BIBLIOGRAPHY

Every child of God is precious to the Lord and deeply loved. And every child as a servant of the Lord touches the lives of those who come in contact with him or his ministry. The writing ministries of the following servants have touched this work, and we are grateful that God brought their writings our way. We hereby acknowledge their ministry to us, being fully aware that there are many others down through the years whose writings have touched our lives and who deserve mention, but whose names have faded from our memory. May our wonderful Lord continue to bless the ministries of these dear servants—and the ministries of us all—as we diligently labor to reach the world for Christ and to meet the desperate needs of those who suffer so much.

THE GREEK SOURCES

Expositor's Greek Testament, Edited by W. Robertson Nicoll. Grand Rapids, MI: Eerdmans Publishing Co., 1970.

Robertson, A.T. *Word Pictures in the New Testament*. Nashville, TN: Broadman Press, 1930.

Thayer, Joseph Henry. *Greek-English Lexicon of the New Testament*. New York: American Book Co., n.d.

Vincent, Marvin R. *Word Studies in the New Testament*. Grand Rapids, MI: Eerdmans Publishing Co., 1969.

Vine, W.E. *Expository Dictionary of New Testament Words*. Old Tappan, NJ: Fleming H. Revell Co., n.d.

Wuest, Kenneth S. *Word Studies in the Greek New Testament*. Grand Rapids, MI: Eerdmans Publishing Co., 1966.

THE REFERENCE WORKS

Cruden's Complete Concordance of the Old & New Testament. Philadelphia, PA: The John C. Winston Co., 1930.

Josephus, Flavius. *Complete Works*. Grand Rapids, MI: Kregel Publications, 1981.

Lockyer, Herbert. *All the Books and Chapters of the Bible*. Grand Rapids, MI: Zondervan Publishing House, 1966.

_____. *All the Kings and Queens of the Bible*. Grand Rapids, MI: Zondervan Publishing House, 1961.

_____. *All the Men of the Bible*. Grand Rapids, MI: Zondervan Publishing House, 1958.

_____. *All the Miracles of the Bible*. Grand Rapids, MI: Zondervan Publishing House, 1961.

_____. *All the Parables of the Bible*. Grand Rapids, MI: Zondervan Publishing House, 1963.

_____. *The Women of the Bible*. Grand Rapids, MI: Zondervan Publishing House, 1967.

Nave, Orville J. *Nave's Topical Bible*. Nashville, TN: The Southwestern Company. Copyright © by J.B. Henderson, 1921.

The Amplified Bible. Scripture taken from *THE AMPLIFIED BIBLE*, Old Testament copyright © 1965, 1987 by the Zondervan Publishing House. *The Amplified New Testament* copyright © 1958, 1987 by The Lockman Foundation. Used by permission.

The Four Translation New Testament (Including King James, New American Standard, Williams - New Testament in the Language of the People, Beck - New Testament in the Language of Today.) Minneapolis, MN: World Wide Publications.

The New Compact Bible Dictionary, Edited by T. Alton Bryant. Grand Rapids, MI: Zondervan Publishing House, 1967.

The New Thompson Chain Reference Bible. Indianapolis, IN: B.B. Kirkbride Bible Co., Inc., 1964.

THE COMMENTARIES

Barclay, William. *Daily Study Bible Series*. Philadelphia, PA: Westminster Press, Began in 1953.

Bruce, F.F. *The Epistle to the Ephesians*. Westwood, NJ: Fleming H. Revell Co., 1968.

_____. *Epistle to the Hebrews*. Grand Rapids, MI: Eerdmans Publishing Co., 1964.

_____. *The Epistles of John*. Old Tappan, NJ: Fleming H. Revell Co., 1970.

THE COMMENTARIES (continued)

Criswell, W.A. *Expository Sermons on Revelation*. Grand Rapids, MI: Zondervan Publishing House, 1962-66.

Greene, Oliver. *The Epistles of John*. Greenville, SC: The Gospel Hour, Inc., 1966.

_____. *The Epistles of Paul the Apostle to the Hebrews*. Greenville, SC: The Gospel Hour, Inc., 1965.

_____. *The Epistles of Paul the Apostle to Timothy & Titus*. Greenville, SC: The Gospel Hour, Inc., 1964.

_____. *The Revelation Verse by Verse Study*. Greenville, SC: The Gospel Hour, Inc., 1963.

Henry, Matthew. *Commentary on the Whole Bible*. Old Tappan, NJ: Fleming H. Revell Co.

Hodge, Charles. *Exposition on Romans & on Corinthians*. Grand Rapids, MI: Eerdmans Publishing Co., 1972-1973.

Ladd, George Eldon. *A Commentary On the Revelation of John*. Grand Rapids, MI: Eerdmans Publishing Co., 1972-1973.

Leupold, H.C. *Exposition of Daniel*. Grand Rapids, MI: Baker Book House, 1969.

Morris, Leon. *The Gospel According to John*. Grand Rapids, MI: Eerdmans Publishing Co., 1971.

Newell, William R. *Hebrews, Verse by Verse*. Chicago, IL: Moody Press, 1947.

Strauss, Lehman. *Devotional Studies in Galatians & Ephesians*. Neptune, NJ: Loizeaux Brothers, 1957.

_____. *Devotional Studies in Philippians*. Neptune, NJ: Loizeaux Brothers, 1959.

_____. *James, Your Brother*. Neptune, NJ: Loizeaux Brothers, 1956.

_____. *The Book of the Revelation*. Neptune, NJ: Loizeaux Brothers, 1964.

The New Testament & Wycliffe Bible Commentary, Edited by Charles F. Pfeiffer & Everett F. Harrison. New York: The Iverson Associates, 1971. Produced for Moody Monthly. Chicago Moody Press, 1962.

The Pulpit Commentary, Edited by H.D.M. Spence & Joseph S. Exell. Grand Rapids, MI: Eerdmans Publishing Co., 1950.

Thomas, W.H. Griffith. *Hebrews, A Devotional Commentary*. Grand Rapids, MI: Eerdmans Publishing Co., 1970.

_____. *Outline Studies in the Acts of the Apostles*. Grand Rapids, MI: Eerdmans Publishing Co., 1956.

_____. *St. Paul's Epistle to the Romans*. Grand Rapids, MI: Eerdmans Publishing Co., 1946.

_____. *Studies in Colossians & Philemon*. Grand Rapids, MI: Baker Book House, 1973.

Tyndale New Testament Commentaries. Grand Rapids, MI: Eerdmans Publishing Co., Began in 1958.

Walker, Thomas. *Acts of the Apostles*. Chicago, IL: Moody Press, 1965.

Walvoord, John. *The Thessalonian Epistles*. Grand Rapids, MI: Zondervan Publishing House, 1973.

"Woe is unto me, if I
preach not the gospel"
(1 Co.9:16)

OUTLINE OF HEBREWS
(CHAPTER 11:1-40)

THE PREACHER'S OUTLINE & SERMON BIBLE® is *unique*. It differs from all other Study Bibles & Sermon Resource Materials in that every Passage and Subject is outlined right beside the Scripture. When you choose any *Subject* below and turn to the reference, you have not only the Scripture, but you discover the Scripture and Subject *already outlined for you—verse by verse*.

IV. **THE SUPREME AUTHOR OF FAITH: JESUS CHRIST, GOD'S SON, 10:19–11:40**
- D. The Description of Faith, 11:1-6
- E. Noah's Faith: A Fearful, Reverent Faith, 11:7
- F. Abraham's Faith (Part I): An Obedient, Hopeful Faith, 11:8-10
- G. Sarah's Faith: An Impossible Faith, 11:11-12
- H. The Patriarch's Faith: A Pilgrim's Faith, 11:13-16
- I. Abraham's Faith (Part II): A Sacrificial Faith, 11:17-19
- J. Isaac's Faith: A Strong, Futuristic Faith, 11:20
- K. Jacob's Faith: A Worshipping Faith, 11:21
- L. Joseph's Faith: An Undying Faith, 11:22
- M. Moses' Parent's Faith: A Loving, Fearless Faith, 11:23
- N. Moses Faith: A Self-Denying Faith, 11:24-28
- O. Israel's Faith (Part I): A Delivering Faith, 11:29
- P. Israel's Faith (Part II): A Conquering Faith, 11:30
- Q. Rahab's Faith: A Saving Faith, 11:31
- R. The Great Believers' Faith (Part I): A Heroic Faith, 11:32-34
- S. The Great Believers' Faith (Part II): An Enduring Faith, 11:35-40

| 1. The meaning of faith
  a. The surety of one's hope
  b. The conviction of things not
    seen
2. The reward of faith: God's
  approval
3. The basic understanding of
  faith: God made the world

4. The spiritual power of faith
  a. Illustrated by Abel: The | CHAPTER 11

D. The Description of Faith,
  11:1-6

Now faith is the substance of things hoped for, the evidence of things not seen.
2 For by it the elders obtained a good report.
3 Through faith we understand that the worlds were framed by the word of God, so that things which are seen were not made of things which do appear.
4 By faith Abel offered unto God a more excellent | sacrifice than Cain, by which he obtained witness that he was righteous, God testifying of his gifts: and by it he being dead yet speaketh.
5 By faith Enoch was translated that he should not see death; and was not found, because God had translated him: for before his translation he had this testimony, that he pleased God.
6 But without faith it is impossible to please him: for he that cometh to God must believe that he is, and that he is a rewarder of them that diligently seek him. | power to be counted righteous

b. Illustrated by Enoch: The power to walk with God & to be delivered from death

5. The necessary beliefs of faith[DS1]
  a. Must believe that God exists
  b. Must believe that God rewards the diligent seeker |

DIVISION IV

THE SUPREME AUTHOR OF FAITH: JESUS CHRIST, GOD'S SON, 10:19–11:40

D.   The Description of Faith, 11:1-6

(11:1-6) **Introduction**: this is one of the great chapters in the Bible. It is known as *God's Great Hall of Fame*. Men and women who have *believed* God down through the centuries are listed as being great men and women of God. The key to greatness with God is faith; the person who truly believes God is *great* in the eyes of God. The first part of this great chapter gives us an overall study of faith. It is the *description of faith*.

    1. The meaning of faith (v.1).
    2. The reward of faith: God's approval (v.2).
    3. The basic understanding of faith: God made the world (v.3).
    4. The spiritual power of faith (vv.4-5).
    5. The necessary beliefs of faith (v.6).

1 (11:1) **Faith**: the meaning of faith. What does faith mean? This is the only time the Bible ever defines faith. Time and again, however, the Bible discusses faith and the great importance of faith. The Bible tells us that we must have faith—we must believe God—and it tells us the great things that happen to those who believe God. The Bible also gives example after example of men and women who have and have not believed God and shows in clear terms what happened to each. But, as stated, nowhere does the Bible define faith except here. Therefore, it is important that we clearly grasp this Scripture, understand exactly what faith means. The Biblical definition is this (see He.11:1 in each of the following author's commentaries for their discussion):

      "Now faith is the substance of things hoped for, the evidence of things not seen" (v.1).
      "Now faith is the assurance of things hoped for, the conviction of things not seen" (v.1, New American Standard).
      "Now faith is the assurance of the things we hope for, the proof of the reality of the things we cannot see" (v.1, Williams).
      "Faith is being sure of the things we hope for, being convinced of the things we can't see" (v.1, Beck).
      "Now faith is the assurance (the confirmation, the title-deed) of the things [we] hope for, being the proof of things [we] do not see and the conviction of their reality—faith perceiving as real fact what is not revealed to the senses" (v.1, Amplified New Testament).
      "Now faith is the title deed of things hoped for, the conviction of things which are not being seen" (Kenneth Wuest).
      "Faith means that we are certain of the things we hope for, convinced of the things we do not see" (William Barclay).
      "Faith is a hope that is absolutely certain that what it believes is true, and that what it expects will come" (Barclay says this is what faith is to the writer of Hebrews).
      "Faith is trust in the unseen. It is not trust in the unknown, for we may know by faith what we cannot see with the eye" (Wycliffe Bible Commentary).
      "Faith apprehends as a real fact what is not revealed to the senses. It rests on the fact, acts upon it, and is upheld by it in the face of all that seems to contradict it. Faith is a real seeing" (Marvin Vincent).
      "Faith is the substance, the foundation, the title deed, the assurance of things hoped for" (Oliver Greene).

Matthew Henry, one of God's great servants of a former generation, makes some excellent statements that are well worth our thought:

> Faith and hope go together; and the same things that are the object of our hope are the object of our faith.
>
> It [faith] is a firm persuasion and expectation that God will perform all that He has promised to us in Christ; and this persuasion is so strong that it gives the soul...*possession*...of those things.
>
> Believers in the exercise of faith are filled with joy unspeakable and full of glory. Christ dwells in the soul by faith; and the soul is filled with the fullness of God.[1]

Now, what is faith? Look at the Biblical definition again.

"Now faith is the substance of things hoped for, the evidence of things not seen" (v.1).

The word "substance" (hupostasis) means the foundation, assurance, title-deed, and guarantee of things hoped for. The word "evidence" (elegchos) means conviction.

According to most commentators, this is what is meant by these two words. Therefore, faith would be defined as:

> Now faith is the assurance of things hoped for, the conviction of things not seen.

Look closely at what is being said and note that faith is being described as an act, an act of the mind and heart. That is, our heart and mind believe something and we have assurance and conviction that it is true. This is certainly true; faith is an act of the mind and heart. But many of the earlier interpreters understood "substance" (hupostasis) to mean *real being, substantial nature, the real nature of a thing*. Vincent points this out and even says that it suggests the real sense, but he backs off of the meaning and concludes that faith is basically an act of what he calls "moral intelligence directed at an object."[2]

This is not to argue with God's dear servants who stress that faith is primarily an act of the mind and heart. It is only to say that Scripture seems to be saying that faith is more than an act. Scripture seems to be saying that faith is the *actual possession* of reality. Is this not what the definition "title-deed" is saying? The person who holds the title-deed to property actually *possesses* the property. It is his already. Certainly from God's perspective, we already possess His promises; He has already seated us in the heavenlies, and we already possess eternal life. It is not that we are going to possess it; we already possess it. The point is this: holding the title-deed to property and possessing something is more than assurance and conviction. It is possessing reality, actually holding something that is substantial and real. It is possessing the land, the promises of God. Faith is possessing the substance of the promises of God, the evidence of things not seen. If I possess them, the substance is there; the evidence is there. The substance and evidence, the fact that I already possess them, are my assurance and conviction. This is important to note and bears repeating: the substance and evidence, the fact that I already possess eternal life, is the basis of my assurance and conviction, of never experiencing death.

Now, what does all this discussion mean? It means this: faith is the *substance, the actual possession*, of things hoped for, the *evidence and reality* of things not seen. It is *both an act and a possession* of the thing believed. It is believing and trusting in that which actually exists—in that which we can possess. We may not be able to see it, but it is real and existing, and we can possess it by believing and having faith in it. We can possess it now—we cannot see it, but we can actually possess the very substance of it by believing and entrusting our lives to it.

⇒ Faith is *trusting and possessing* all that God is and says.

⇒ Faith is *believing and possessing* all that God is and says.

⇒ Faith is *having confidence in and possessing* all that God is and says.

⇒ Faith is *hoping for something and possessing it* because God is (exists) and has promised it.

Thought 1. Note what Biblical faith is not. It is not...

• "I think so, I hope so."

• "It may be so; it may not be so."

• "It might be true; it might not be true."

Biblical faith does not deal with what is unreal, imaginary, fanciful, visionary, superficial, or deceptive. Biblical faith is the knowledge, experience, and *possession* of things hoped for. True Biblical faith deals only with truth and reality. It is...

• knowing what is real

• experiencing what is real

• possessing what is real

---

[1] Matthew Henry. *Matthew Henry's Commentary,* Vol.6. (Old Tappan, NJ: Fleming H. Revell Co., n.d.), p.938.

[2] Marvin Vincent. *Word Studies in the New Testament*, Vol.4. (Grand Rapids, MI: Eerdmans Publishing Co., 1969), p.510.

2 (11:2) **Faith**: the reward of faith. What is the reward of faith? God's approval. God is pleased, very pleased, when we believe Him and His promises. This is the point of this verse. The elders, great men of God who lived in the past, believed God and followed God. They turned away from the world and its possessions and pleasures and followed God. They believed God, that He had much more to offer—that His promises of an eternal land and of eternal life were true. Therefore they staked their lives, all they were and had, upon that hope. And their faith in God pleased God to no end. Therefore, God accepted their faith and has honored them because of it. He has, of course, honored them by recording their faith in His Word and using their example as a challenge to believers of every generation. But God has also honored them by fulfilling their faith; God has taken them on home to be with Him.

Thought 1. The reward of faith is God's approval, and when God approves us, He accepts us into His eternal presence. This simply means that God looks after and cares for us, giving us victory over all the enemies of this world—including death—and He does it for eternity. The approval of God means that God fulfills all His promises to us. The promises of God become a living reality in our experiences, both daily and eternally.

"That whosoever believeth in him should not perish, but have eternal life. For God so loved the world, that he gave his only begotten Son, that whosoever believeth in him should not perish, but have everlasting life" (Jn.3:15-16).

"Verily, verily, I say unto you, He that heareth my word, and believeth on him that sent me, hath everlasting life, and shall not come into condemnation; but is passed from death unto life" (Jn.5:24).

"Then came he to Derbe and Lystra: and, behold, a certain disciple was there, named Timotheus, the son of a certain woman, which was a Jewess, and believed; but his father was a Greek: which was well reported of by the brethren that were at Lystra and Iconium" (Ac.16:1-2).

"First, I thank my God through Jesus Christ for you all, that your faith is spoken of throughout the whole world" (Ro.1:8).

"And we have sent with him [Titus] the brother, whose praise is in the gospel throughout all the churches" (2 Co.8:18).

"To the praise of the glory of his grace, wherein he hath made us accepted in the beloved. In whom we have redemption through his blood, the forgiveness of sins, according to the riches of his grace" (Ep.1:6-7).

"Demetrius hath good report of all men, and of the truth itself: yea, and we also bear record; and ye know that our record is true" (3 Jn.12).

3 (11:3) **Faith—Creation**: the basic understanding of faith—that God has made the world. Note the word "understanding" (noeo). It means to perceive with the mind, to understand, to know a true fact. Some say the belief that God made the world is only an assumption, that it is the beginning point in building the Christian's beliefs and theology. There is both truth and error in this charge. The error is found in the word assumption. The truth is this: the Christian begins with a fact that is true: *God did create the world*. The Christian believer's starting point is more than an assumption—it is an understanding, a true fact, the very basic fact that God did create the world. This understanding is based upon four things:

⇒ The world itself: looking at and observing the world, and studying and thinking about its origin, purpose, and end.

⇒ The Bible, the Word of God, the written revelation of God.

⇒ The Lord Jesus Christ, the living revelation of God.

⇒ The witness of the Holy Spirit who is given to every believer. He bears witness that Jesus Christ and the Word of God are true. This is critical, for it is *a fact*, as any true Christian believer can testify. When a person believes in the Lord Jesus Christ, God puts His Spirit into the heart and life of the deliver. The Holy Spirit seals, guarantees, bears witness that Jesus Christ is the Son of God and that the promises and teachings of God's Word are true.

The point is this: the Christian believer has four strong sources that show the origin, purpose, and end of all things; and all four are undeniable. How can this be said? How can we say that these witnesses are undeniable?

⇒ Because we can look and observe the world. The world is real; it is truth. The world does exist.

⇒ Because we can look and observe the Bible, its teachings and promises at work in human lives—the lives of those who believe it. The Word of God sitting there and working itself out in lives is real. The Word of God is truth; it is absolutely true that it exists and works in human lives just as it claims.

⇒ Because we can know the Lord Jesus Christ through a study of the records of His life. He lived, and the fact that He lived is truth. But we can also see that the very things He claimed are at work in human lives. Jesus Christ can be studied and known in the lives of those who truly believe and follow Him. For Jesus Christ lives in the lives of true believers and followers of His.

⇒ Because we can know and see the work of the Holy Spirit in lives as discussed above.

Again, the believer has four strong witnesses that bear testimony that God is—that He exists and that He has created the worlds. Where did the worlds come from? A chart is probably the best way to grasp what the believer understands as opposed to what the unbeliever understands.

When a believer looks at the origin of the world, he sees...	*When an unbeliever looks at the origin of the world, he sees...*
1. God	1. Nothing—absolutely nothing
2. God's Word—God willed and spoke	2. Nothing—absolutely nothing
3. Matter appeared, the worlds were created by God's Word	3. Matter appeared; some gas or force formed out of absolutely nothing
4. The things seen were made by God	4. The things seen were made by just appearing out of absolutely nothing

The point is this: we were not here when God created the world, but we *believe* that a Supreme Being, God Himself, created the world.

⇒ The world says that a Designer made the world.

⇒ The Bible, the Word of God, says that God made the world.

⇒ Jesus Christ says that God made the world.

⇒ The Holy Spirit bears witness to the believer's heart that the claims and promises of the Word of God are true.

Therefore, the basic understanding of the believer is that God is (exists) and that He has created the world. God is the Person who is behind life and the world of life. God gave breath to man and His world. He made the things that are seen.

Thought 1. Matthew Henry has an excellent exposition on this point that merits our study.

> *By faith we understand much more of the formation of the world than ever could be understood by the naked eye of natural reason. Faith is not a force upon the understanding, but a friend and a help to it. Now what does faith give us to understand concerning the worlds?...*
>
> *1. That these worlds were not eternal, nor did they produce themselves, but they were made by another.*
>
> *2. That the maker of the worlds is God: he is the maker of all things.*
>
> *3. That he made the world with great exactness; it was a framed work, in everything duly adapted and disposed to answer its end.*
>
> *4. That God made the world by his word, that is, by his essential wisdom and eternal Son, and by his active will, saying, Let it be done, and it was done, Ps.33.*
>
> *5. That the world was thus framed out of nothing, out of no pre-existent matter...[by] God, who can call things that are not as if they were, and command them into being. These things we understand by faith.*
>
> *The Bible gives us the truest and most exact account of the origin of all things, and we are to believe it, and not to wrest or run down the scripture-account of the creation, because it does not suit with some fantastic hypotheses of our own, which has been in some learned but conceited men the first remarkable step towards infidelity, and has led them into many more.*[3]

Thought 2. William Barclay also has his usual practical comments that are helpful in the personal application of this point to our lives.

> *The writer to the Hebrews goes further. He says that it is an act of faith to believe that God made this world. Then he goes on to say that the things which are seen emerged from the things which are not seen. Now when he said that he was aiming a blow at current belief. It was current belief that God created the world out of already existing matter, and not out of nothing. Further, it was current belief that this existing matter was flawed and that therefore from the beginning this is a flawed world because it is made from flawed material. The writer to the Hebrews insists that God did not work with existing material; God created the world from nothing. Now when he argued like this he was not interested in cosmological speculation. He was not interested in the scientific side of the matter. What he wanted to stress was the fact that this is God's world. If we can grip the fact that this is God's world, that God is responsible for it, then two things follow. First, we will use it as such. We will remember that everything in it is God's and we will try to use it as God would have us use it. Second, we will remember that, even when it does not look like it, somehow God is in control. If we believe that this is God's world then there comes the faith and the hope which enable us to do the most difficult thing in the world—to accept what we cannot understand. If we believe that this is God's world then into life there comes a new sense of responsibility*

---

[3] *Matthew Henry's Commentary*, Vol.6, p.938.

and into life there comes a new power of acceptance, for everything belongs to God, and all is in the hands of God.[4]

"In the beginning God created the heaven and the earth" (Ge.1:1).

"Thou, even thou, art Lord alone; thou hast made heaven, the heaven of heavens, with all their host, the earth, and all things that are therein, the seas, and all that is therein, and thou preservest them all; and the host of heaven worshippeth thee" (Ne.9:6).

"He stretcheth out the north over the empty place, and hangeth the earth upon nothing" (Jb.26:7).

"For he hath founded it upon the seas, and established it upon the floods" (Ps.24:2).

"By the word of the LORD were the heavens made; and all the host of them by the breath of his mouth" (Ps.33:6).

"The sea is his, and he made it: and his hands formed the dry land" (Ps.95:5).

"Of old hast thou laid the foundation of the earth: and the heavens are the work of thy hands" (Ps.102:25).

"Who laid the foundations of the earth, that it should not be removed for ever" (Ps.104:5).

"And when they heard that, they lifted up their voice to God with one accord, and said, Lord, thou art God, which hast made heaven, and earth, and the sea, and all that in them is" (Ac.4:24).

"Hath not my hand made all these things?" (Ac.7:50).

"And saying, Sirs, why do ye these things? We also are men of like passions with you, and preach unto you that ye should turn from these vanities unto the living God, which made heaven, and earth, and the sea, and all things that are therein" (Ac.14:15).

"Through faith we understand that the worlds were framed by the word of God, so that things which are seen were not made of things which do appear" (He.11:3).

4 (11:4-5) **Faith, Power of—Abel—Enoch—Cain**: the spiritual power of faith. The power of faith is the message of the glorious gospel, the glorious hope that God has given from the beginning of time. The power is twofold and it is given in the most meaningful way possible, by showing how the power takes effect in the lives of believers. Two believers who experienced the power of faith were Abel and Enoch.

1. Faith has the power to be counted as righteousness. No greater gift could be given us than to give us the glorious privilege of being counted righteous by God.

⇒ To be counted righteous is the great need of man, for we are not righteous. And unless some way can be found to cause God to count us righteous, we shall never be allowed to live with God.

Abel tells us there is a way to be counted righteous. How? By approaching and worshipping God exactly like He says, that is, by the sacrifice of blood. What does this mean?

When Adam and Eve sinned, they became aware of their nakedness. Nakedness is a symbol of their being aware and conscious of sin (see Ge.3:9-10). God loved them; therefore, He provided clothing to cover their nakedness. Note what the clothing was. It was coats or skins from animals, a symbol that sin had to be covered by the shedding of blood. This was a symbol that pointed to the blood of Jesus Christ, the blood of God's Son, that had to be shed in order to cover the sins of men.

The point is this: from the very first parents on earth, God laid it down that the sin and guilt of man had to be borne by either man himself or by a substitute. Man had to die for his own sins or else a substitute had to be sacrificed for his sins. Adam and Eve taught this to their children. Note what happened.

"And Adam knew Eve his wife; and she conceived, and bare Cain, and said, I have gotten a man from the LORD. And she again bare his brother Abel. And Abel was a keeper of sheep, but Cain was a tiller of the ground. And in process of time it came to pass, that Cain brought of the fruit of the ground an offering unto the LORD. And Abel, he also brought of the firstlings of his flock and of the fat thereof. And the LORD had respect unto Abel and to his offering: but unto Cain and to his offering he had not respect. And Cain was very wroth, and his countenance fell. And the LORD said unto Cain, Why are thou wroth? and why is thy countenance fallen? If thou doest well, shalt thou not be accepted? and if thou doest not well, sin lieth at the door. And unto thee shall be his desire, and thou shalt rule over him. And Cain talked with Abel his brother: and it came to pass, when they were in the field, that Cain rose up against Abel his brother, and slew him" (Ge.4:1-8).

"By faith Abel offered unto God a more excellent sacrifice than Cain, by which he obtained witness that he was righteous, God testifying of his gifts: and by it he being dead yet speaketh" (He.11:4).

The difference between the two offerings was this: Abel believed God and approached and worshipped God exactly as God said: through the sacrifice of another, the sacrifice of an animal. But Cain did not believe God. He did not accept God's Word; he did not approach God through the sacrifice of another. He made a material sacrifice and offering to God:

---

4 William Barclay. *The Letter to the Hebrews.* "The Daily Study Bible." (Philadelphia, PA: Westminster Press, 1957), p.147f.

he approached God through money and earthly gifts, through the efforts and fruits of human works, the fruit borne of the earth, the fruit borne by his own human, frail, aging, and dying hands.

Very simply, Abel believed God. He recognized just what Scripture says: that he was sinful and imperfect and that he could never be acceptable to God who is perfect and holy, not until his sins and their guilt had been paid for and removed. Abel knew that his sins had to be removed—that he had to be counted righteous before he could ever be accepted by God. Therefore, he believed God would count him righteous if he let another bear his sins for him. He believed exactly what Scripture proclaims to us.

"[Jesus Christ] who his own self bare our sins in his own body on the tree, that we, being dead to sins, should live unto righteousness: by whose stripes ye were healed" (1 Pe.2:24).
"For Christ also hath once suffered for sins, the just for the unjust, that he might bring us to God, being put to death in the flesh, but quickened by the Spirit" (1 Pe.3:18).

This is the power of faith: faith gives us the power to be counted righteous.

"And he [Abraham] believed in the LORD; and he counted it to him for righteousness" (Ge.15:6).
"And by him all that believe are justified from all things, from which ye could not be justified by the law of Moses" (Acts 13:39).
"For all have sinned, and come short of the glory of God; being justified freely by his grace through the redemption that is in Christ Jesus" (Ro.3:23-24).
"For what saith the scripture? Abraham believed God, and it was counted unto him for righteousness" (Ro.4:3).
"Therefore being justified by faith, we have peace with God through our Lord Jesus Christ" (Ro.5:1).
"Much more then, being now justified by his blood, we shall be saved from wrath through him" (Ro.5:9).
"For he that is dead [counted dead, justified] is freed from sin" (Ro.6:7).
"Who shall lay any thing to the charge of God's elect? It is God that justifieth" (Ro.8:33).
"And such were some of you: but ye are washed, but ye are sanctified, but ye are justified in the name of the Lord Jesus, and by the Spirit of our God" (1 Co.6:11).
"Knowing that a man is not justified by the works of the law, but by the faith of Jesus Christ, even we have believed in Jesus Christ, that we might be justified by the faith of Christ, and not by the works of the law: for by the works of the law shall no flesh be justified" (Ga.2:16).
"Even as Abraham believed God, and it was accounted to him for righteousness" (Ga.3:6).
"Wherefore the law was our schoolmaster to bring us unto Christ, that we might be justified by faith" (Ga.3:24).
"And be found in him, not having mine own righteousness, which is of the law, but that which is through the faith of Christ, the righteousness which is of God by faith" (Ph.3:9).

Thought 1. Note that Cain approached God; he was religious. But his religion was a formal religion:
⇒ a religion of ritual, form, and ceremony.
⇒ a religion of personal sacrifice and works, of doing good and even of sacrificing in order to do good.
⇒ a religion of man, of his own choosing, of his own ideas and imaginations as to how he was to approach God.

What an indictment of so many religions! What a challenge to search our hearts and lives to make sure that we are worshipping God through His own dear Son who died for our sins.

2. Faith has the power to give us a day by day walk with God and to deliver us from death. What a glorious gift: the presence and power of God as we walk day by day and the eternal deliverance from death. Enoch illustrates this:

"And Enoch walked with God: and he was not; for God took him" (Ge.5:24).
"By faith Enoch was translated that he should not see death; and was not found, because God had translated him: for before his translation he had this testimony, that he pleased God" (He.11:5).

Enoch believed God, believed that if he walked and fellowshipped with God day by day then God would look after and care for him. Therefore Enoch walked with God and God looked after and cared for him. God even conquered death for Enoch. When Enoch was ready to go home to God, God transferred him right on into heaven, right into God's very own presence. Enoch experienced the promise that is made to every believer: we shall never taste or experience death.
⇒ Enoch's faith gave him a day by day walk with God—the knowledge and fellowship, care and provision, protection and deliverance of God.

"Abide in me, and I in you. As the branch cannot bear fruit of itself, except it abide in the vine; no more can ye, except ye abide in me. I am the vine, ye are the branches: He that abideth in me, and I in him, the same bringeth forth much fruit: for without me ye can do nothing. If a man abide not in me, he is cast forth as a branch, and is withered; and men gather them, and cast them into the fire, and they are burned. If ye abide in me, and my words abide in you, ye shall ask what ye will, and it shall be done unto you" (Jn.15:4-7).

"That they should seek the Lord, if haply they might feel after him, and find him, though he be not far from every one of us" (Acts 17:27).

"God is faithful, by whom ye were called unto the fellowship of his Son Jesus Christ our Lord" (1 Co.1:9).

"As ye have therefore received Christ Jesus the Lord, so walk ye in him" (Col.2:6).

"Draw nigh to God, and he will draw nigh to you. Cleanse your hands, ye sinners; and purify your hearts, by double minded" (Js.4:8).

"That which we have seen and heard declare we unto you, that ye also may have fellowship with us: and truly our fellowship is with the Father, and with his Son Jesus Christ" (1 Jn.1:3).

"He that saith he abideth in him ought himself also so to walk, even as he walked" (1 Jn.2:6).

"Behold, I stand at the door, and knock: if any man hear my voice, and open the door, I will come in to him, and will sup with him, and he with me" (Re.3:20).

"The LORD is nigh unto them that are of a broken heart; and saveth such as be of a contrite spirit" (Ps.34:18).

"The LORD is nigh unto all them that call upon him, to all that call upon him in truth" (Ps.145:18).

⇒ Enoch's faith gave him the longed for deliverance from death.

"And as Moses lifted up the serpent in the wilderness, even so must the Son of man be lifted up: that whosoever believeth in him should not perish, but have eternal life" (Jn.3:14-15).

"For God so loved the world, that he gave his only begotten Son, that whosoever believeth in him should not perish, but have everlasting life" (Jn.3:16).

"He that believeth on the Son hath everlasting life: and he that believeth not the Son shall not see life; but the wrath of God abideth on him" (Jn.3:36).

"Then said the Jews unto him [Christ], Now we know that thou hast a devil. Abraham is dead, and the prophets; and thou sayest, If a man keep my saying, he shall never taste of death" (Jn.8:52).

"And this is life eternal, that they might know thee the only true God, and Jesus Christ, whom thou hast sent" (Jn.17:3).

"But we see Jesus, who was made a little lower than the angels for the suffering of death, crowned with glory and honour that he by the grace of God should taste death for every man" (He.2:9).

"For he that soweth to his flesh shall of the flesh reap corruption; but he that soweth to the Spirit shall of the Spirit reap life everlasting" (Ga.6:8).

Thought 1. Oliver Greene has an excellent application on Enoch that stirs the glorious hope of conquering death:

It has been said that Enoch was walking with God one day, and they walked and talked so long in such sweet fellowship that near nightfall God said to Enoch, "It is nearer to my house than to your house, so let us go on to my house." That is a wonderful way to think about it, but the Bible simply tells us that "Enoch walked with God, and was not, for God took him,"

...the record of Enoch, though very brief, is in a very unique place in the Word of God. In Genesis 5, beginning with verse 5, we read:

"And all the days that Adam lived were nine hundred and thirty years - AND HE DIED."

"And all the days of Seth were nine hundred and twelve years - AND HE DIED" (v.8).

"And all the days of Enos were nine hundred and five years - AND HE DIED" (v.11).

"And all the days of Cainan were nine hundred and ten years - AND HE DIED" (v.14).

"And all the days of Mahalaleel were eight hundred ninety and five years - AND HE DIED" (v.17).

"And all the days of Jared were nine hundred sixty and two years - AND HE DIED" (v.20).

"And all the days of ENOCH were three hundred sixty and five years: and Enoch walked with God, AND HE WAS NOT, OR GOD TOOK HIM" (vv.23,24).

"And all the days of Methuselah were nine hundred sixty and nine years - AND HE DIED" (v.27).

"And all the days of Lamech were seven hundred seventy and seven years - AND HE DIED" (v.31).

From these passages we note that Enoch lived in one of the darkest periods of human history, he lived in the midst of dying men, and yet he did not die. He was translated; God took him to heaven - alive.

Enoch is definitely a type of the New Testament saints who will be translated when the church is caught up to meet the Lord in the air, in the midst of an age of wholesale death and in an hour darker than any yet known to man! Surely that hour is upon us. Surely these are the days known as "the beginning of sorrows." The darkest hour is always just before dawn, and surely the night is far spent. Surely Jesus will come quickly. We do not know the day or the hour of His coming, but we do believe He is coming soon.[5]

---

5   Oliver Greene. *The Epistle of Paul the Apostle to the Hebrews.* (Greenville, SC: The Gospel Hour, 1965), p.448f.

5 **(11:6) Faith—God, Existence**: the necessary beliefs of faith. This is one of the great verses of Scripture, a verse that should be memorized and held within the heart of every believer, layman as well as minister:

> **"But without faith it is impossible to please him: for he that cometh to God must believe that he is, and that he is a rewarder of them that diligently seek him" (v.6).**

1. It is impossible to please God without faith. By faith is meant a living, active faith, a faith that knows and follows God, communes and fellowships with God. It does not matter what a person does; without faith he cannot please God. It is utterly impossible to please God without faith. What does this mean? The person will never be acceptable to God nor accepted by God. Without faith the person will never live with God, not in this world nor in the next world. Without faith, a person has to plow through this life all alone and handle all the trials, temptations, sufferings, accidents, diseases, and death by himself. Without faith, a person stands all alone in this world—utterly without God. It is impossible for him to please God. The Greek scholar Kenneth Wuest says:

> *The writer lays down an axiomatic truth. He uses the aorist tense in the infinitive "to please." The statement is universal in its application and timeless. The idea is, "Without faith it is impossible to please Him at all."*[6]

> **"Verily, Verily, I say unto thee, We speak that we do know, and testify that we have seen; and ye receive not our witness" (Jn.3:11).**
> **"He that believeth on him is not condemned: but he that believeth not is condemned already, because he hath not believed in the name of the only begotten Son of God" (Jn.3:18).**
> **"He that believeth on the Son hath everlasting life: and he that believeth not the Son shall not see life; but the wrath of God abideth on him" (Jn.3:36).**
> **"I said therefore unto you, that ye shall die in your sins: for if ye believe not that I am he, ye shall die in your sins" (Jn.8:24).**
> **"Take heed, brethren, lest there be in any of you an evil heart of unbelief, in departing from the living God" (He.3:12).**

2. The person who comes to God must believe two things.
   a. He *must believe* in God—that God is—that God exists. The words "must believe" (pisteusai dei) mean necessary and essential, absolutely necessary and essential. A.T. Robertson says it is a "moral necessity to have faith....The very Existence of God is a matter of intelligent faith...so that men are left without excuse (Ro.1:19f)."[7]
   ⇒ A person must look at the worlds (heaven and earth) and at himself—at the existence, design, order, and end of all things—and believe in God.
   ⇒ A person must look at the Word of God, the Holy Bible, and believe in God.
   ⇒ A person must look at Jesus Christ, the very Son of God, who reveals God to man, and believe in God.

   b. He must believe that God rewards those who diligently seek Him. Note the word "diligently" (ekzetousin). It means to *seek out God*; to diligently seek to find Him and to follow Him. God does not reward the sleepy-eyed, complacent, non-thinker, half-interested, worldly-minded, pleasure seeker. God rewards those who diligently seek to know and follow Him. The idea is that we must be in earnest and persevere and endure to the end. What is the reward to those who diligently seek God? It is the same reward given to Abel and Enoch: righteousness and God's care in this life and deliverance from death unto eternal life.

> **"And I say unto you, Ask, and it shall be given you: seek, and ye shall find; knock, and it shall be opened unto you. For every one that asketh receiveth; and he that seeketh findeth; and to him that knocketh it shall be opened" (Lu.11:9-10).**
> **"Then said they unto him, What shall we do, that we might work the works of God? Jesus answered and said unto them, This is the work of God, that ye believe on him whom he hath sent" (Jn.6:28-29).**
> **"That they should seek the Lord, if haply they might feel after him, and find him, though he be not far from every one of us" (Ac.17:27).**
> **"So then faith cometh by hearing, and hearing by the word of God" (Ro.10:17).**
> **"And this is his commandment, That we should believe on the name of his Son Jesus Christ, and love one another, as he gave us commandment" (1 Jn.3:23).**
> **"But if from thence thou shalt seek the LORD thy God, thou shalt find him, if thou seek him with all thy heart and with all thy soul" (De.4:29).**
> **"If my people, which are called by my name, shall humble themselves, and pray, and seek my face, and turn from their wicked ways; then will I hear from heaven, and will forgive their sin, and will heal their land" (2 Chr.7:14).**
> **"I love them that love me; and those that seek me early shall find me" (Pr.8:17).**
> **"And ye shall seek me, and find me, when ye shall search for me with all your heart" (Je.29:13).**

---

6 Kenneth Wuest. *Hebrews.* "Word Studies in the Greek New Testament," Vol.2. (Grand Rapids, MI: Eerdmans Publishing Co., 1947), p.198.
7 A.T. Robertson. *Word Pictures in the New Testament*, Vol.5. (Nashville, TN: Broadman Press, 1930), p.420f.

DEEPER STUDY # 1

(11:6) **Faith**: a person can *grow* in faith and power. Faith and power can be developed by doing two things.

1. By practicing hope (He.11:1), that is, by hoping for something and claiming it because God has promised it.
2. By diligently seeking God (He.11:6). Christ tells us what is meant by *diligent seeking*. It means...
   a. To "hunger and thirst after righteousness" (Mt.5:6).
   b. To "ask...seek...knock" (Mt.7:7-8).
   c. To "seek ye first the kingdom of God and His righteousness" (Mt.6:33).
   d. To "pray and fast," that is, to persevere in prayer (Mt.17:21).

The person who needs something and lives on his face in prayer before God (asking, seeking, and knocking) will experience God answering his need. Thus he will be encouraged to trust God, that is, to seek and knock even more and more. A genuine *faith in God* lives before God. That is what faith is: living before God. Faith is entrusting one's life to God. It is trusting God, depending upon God, believing God, seeking God, conversing with God, sharing with God, and fellowshipping with God. A person who really believes that God exists will do these things.

The greater the need, the greater amount of time *true faith* spends alone with God discussing the need. The greater the need, the more diligent *true faith* seeks the answer to its need.

What happens is this: as a person *diligently seeks* God, he discovers that *true faith* diligently lives before God in prayer and devotion and is given what it hopes for. Therefore the person learns to trust God more and more. He grows in faith.

One thing, however, always needs to be remembered. God is not going to reward sinful, carnal trust, nor is He going to reward a doubting trust. If He answered a doubting trust or a carnal hope and prayer, then the doubting and carnal person would begin to think that the life he is living is acceptable to God. God does not approve sinful and carnal living, nor does He approve a doubting heart. God honors righteous living and a believing heart. It is the person who truly lives righteously and believes enough to diligently seek God who grows and grows in faith (Js.4:3; 1 Co.3:1-3; see Mt.20:21).

	E. Noah's Faith: A Fearful, Reverent Faith,^{DS1} 11:7

1. His faith: A faith that promptly obeyed God—in holy fear
2. His reward
  a. His family was saved
  b. The world was condemned
  c. He was counted righteous
	7 By faith Noah, being warned of God of things not seen as yet, moved with fear, prepared an ark to the saving of his house; by the which he condemned the world, and became heir of the righteousness which is by faith.

DIVISION IV

THE SUPREME AUTHOR OF FAITH: JESUS CHRIST, GOD'S SON, 10:19–11:40

E. Noah's Faith: A Fearful, Reverent Faith, 11:7

(11:7) **Introduction**: Noah stands as a great example in believing God and in believing God's warning of coming judgment. His faith was unique in that it was a fearful, reverent faith.
1. His faith: a faith that promptly obeyed God—in holy fear (v.7).
2. His reward (v.7).

DEEPER STUDY # 1
(11:7-40) **Faith**: this begins the list of the believers included in God's Great Hall of Fame. The first two mentioned, Abel and Enoch, should also be added to it, although they are discussed in the overall description of faith. They illustrate the spiritual power of faith (vv.4-5).

Note: each of the believers illustrate a certain kind of faith. For example, glance at the title of Noah's faith above and it is seen that he illustrates a fearful, reverent faith. A glance at the Outline of Hebrews, pt. IV, will give the reader a quick overview of the various kinds of faith illustrated by the great men and women of God. They stand as dynamic examples to us, a stirring challenge for us to believe God in the midst of a corrupt, godless, and dying world.

Note that many of these are covered in one verse or just a few verses at most. However, they are separated and discussed in separate outlines in order to stress their unique faith. The preacher and teacher may wish to cover several in one message or lesson.

---

1 (11:7) **Noah—Faith**: Noah's faith was a faith that promptly obeyed God—in holy fear (see Ge.5:5-8:22).

> "**By faith Noah, being warned of God of things not seen as yet, moved with fear, prepared an ark to the saving of his house; by the which he condemned the world, and became heir of the righteousness which is by faith**" (v.7).
> "**And God saw that the wickedness of man was great in the earth, and that every imagination of the thoughts of his heart was only evil continually. And it repented the LORD that he had made man on the earth, and it grieved him at his heart. And the LORD said, I will destroy man whom I have created from the face of the earth; both man, and beast, and the creeping thing, and the fowls of the air; for it repenteth me that I have made them. But Noah found grace in the eyes of the LORD....The earth also was corrupt before God, and the earth was filled with violence. And God looked upon the earth, and behold, it was corrupt; for all flesh had corrupted his way upon the earth. And God said unto Noah, The end of all flesh is come before me; for the earth is filled with violence through them; and, behold, I will destroy them with the earth. Make thee an ark of gopher wood; rooms shalt thou make in the ark, and shalt pitch it within and without with pitch....And, behold, I, even I, do bring a flood of waters upon the earth, to destroy all flesh, wherein is the breath of life, from under heaven; and every thing that is in the earth shall die. But with thee will I establish my covenant; and thou shalt come into the ark, thou, and thy sons, and thy wife, and thy sons' wives with thee. And of every living thing of all flesh, two of every sort shalt thou bring into the ark, to keep them alive with thee; they shall be male and female....Thus did Noah; according to all that God commanded him, so did he**" (Ge.6:5-8, 11-14, 17-19, 22).

Note two points about Noah's faith.
1. There was a time back in world history when the earth had become so wicked that it was filled with corruption and violence. It was so corrupt that every imagination of man's heart was corrupt and evil. Man had reached the point of no return; he would never repent and return to God. God was left with no choice: the earth had to be destroyed. But there was one man on earth who was godly—Noah. Noah worshipped and honored God in his life. Therefore, God warned Noah of the coming judgment upon the earth.
  ⇒ God told Noah to prepare an ark and the ark would save him, his family, and two of every animal.
  ⇒ God also told Noah to warn the world of coming judgment.

Note how Noah received the warning from God: he was "moved with fear." The word "fear" (eulabethe) means with godly fear.[1] It has the idea of…

- reverence
- standing in awe of God and His warning
- taking heed lest one fall under God's judgment
- diligently taking God at His Word
- immediately acting upon what God says

Noah believed God's warning of coming judgment, and he began to build the ark with a godly fear and reverence, knowing that what God said would come true. God's judgment would fall upon the earth; Noah believed it and knew it by faith.

Thought 1. God is going to judge the earth a second time—the whole earth, every man and woman. God has warned the earth. His judgment upon the corruption and violence of men is going to fall upon men. We must fear God, fear Him…

- with a godly fear and reverence
- by standing in awe of Him and His warning
- by taking heed lest we fall under His judgment
- by diligently taking Him at His Word
- by immediately acting upon what He has said

Our only hope is to believe God, believe Him with a fearful, reverent faith.

2. Noah stood fast in his faith despite the mockery of the world. Noah lived far, far inland from the ocean; he was nowhere close to the sea or to the shipbuilding yards of the world. Yet, there he was building a ship as large as an ocean liner. Imagine the laughs, mockery, scorn, and abuse Noah suffered. Imagine how often he was called a fool and thought to be insane. But Noah was faithful:

⇒ He preached the righteousness and coming judgment of God. In the eyes of the world he was nothing more than (a *fool preacher*,) but the mockery and abuse did not deter him. He remained faithful and continued to proclaim the truth and to warn the people—all just like God had told him to do.

⇒ He also continued to build the ark—continued to work at saving himself and his own house and as much life as possible upon earth. Noah continued on and on, walking in godly fear, believing the sheer Word of God about coming judgment.

Thought 1. A world that lives by science and technology is tempted to trust in nothing beyond itself. Science and technology tend to draw and focus all attention upon the world of sense and feelings, of comfort, and pleasure, of possessions and self. Therefore, the idea of God and of coming judgment is ignored. And if anyone preaches it, he is ridiculed, mocked, scorned, and often abused. We must be faithful to God, for God *is*. God does exist, and God is going to judge the world.

> "When the Son of man shall come in his glory, and all the holy angels with him, then shall he sit upon the throne of his glory: and before him shall be gathered all nations: and he shall separate them one from another, as a shepherd divideth his sheep from the goats" (Mt.25:31-32).
> "And as it is appointed unto men once to die, but after this the judgment" (He.9:27).
> "The Lord knoweth how to deliver the godly out of temptation, and to reserve the unjust unto the day of judgment to be punished" (2 Pe.2:9).
> "But the heavens and the earth, which are now, by the same word are kept in store, reserved unto fire against the day of judgment and perdition of ungodly men" (2 Pe.3:7).
> "Herein is our love made perfect, that we may have boldness in the day of judgment: because as he is, so are we in this world" (1 Jn.4:17).
> "Behold, the Lord cometh with ten thousands of his saints, to execute judgment upon all, and to convince all that are ungodly among them of all their ungodly deeds which they have ungodly committed, and of all their hard speeches which ungodly sinners have spoken against him" (Jude 14-15).
> "For the Father judgeth no man, but hath committed all judgment unto the Son" (Jn.5:22).
> "And he commanded us to preach unto the people, and to testify that it is he which was ordained of God to be the Judge of quick and dead" (Ac.10:42).
> "Because he hath appointed a day, in the which he will judge the world in righteousness by that man whom he hath ordained; whereof he hath given assurance unto all men, in that he hath raised him from the dead" (Ac.17:31).
> "In the day when God shall judge the secrets of men by Jesus Christ according to my gospel" (Ro.2:16).
> "But why dost thou judge thy brother? or why dost thou set at nought thy brother? for we shall all stand before the judgment seat of Christ" (Ro.14:10).

---

1   A.T. Robertson. *Word Pictures in the New Testament*, Vol.5, p.421.

"I charge thee therefore before God, and the Lord Jesus Christ, who shall judge the quick and the dead at his appearing and his kingdom" (2 Ti.4:1).

"And to you who are troubled rest with us, when the Lord Jesus shall be revealed from heaven with his mighty angels. In flaming fire taking vengeance on them that know not God, and that obey not the gospel of our Lord Jesus Christ" (2 Th.1:7-8).

"Before the LORD: for he cometh, for he cometh to judge the earth: he shall judge the world with righteousness, and the people with his truth" (Ps.96:13).

"I said in mine heart, God shall judge the righteous and the wicked: for there is a time there for every purpose and for every work" (Ec.3:17).

2 (11:7) **Noah—Faith**: Noah's reward was threefold.

1. Noah's house was saved. Noah believed God—believed the warning of God about coming judgment. Therefore, God saved him. Everyone else around Noah died—to be separated from God forever. Why? Because they did not believe God's warning about coming judgment. Note that Noah's whole house was saved. Noah's wife and children were blessed to have a godly father, a father who could teach and guide them into the truth. Remember that his sons had married. The young ladies who had married them had done so despite the stigma of the family being a God-fearing family. They could have married men of the world, but they chose to join the family of God, identifying themselves with the God of God's people. Therefore, God saved them as well as Noah.[2]

2. The world was condemned; that is, Noah's faith was vindicated. The world had mocked and ridiculed Noah's faith and belief in God's warning of judgment. But God vindicated Noah's faith; God judged the world. And the world saw that Noah had been right all the time.

William Barclay states it well:

> *Noah's faith was a judgment on others. That is why, at least in one sense, it is dangerous to be a Christian. It is not that the Christian is self-righteous; it is not that the Christian is censorious; it is not that the Christian goes about finding fault with other people; it is not that the Christian says: "I told you so." It often happens that the Christian simply by being himself is passing judgment on other people. Alcibiades that brilliant, but wild, young man of Athens used to say to Socrates: "Socrates, I hate you, for every time I meet you, you show me what I am." One of the finest men who ever lived in Athens was Aristides, who was called "the just." But they voted to banish and to ostracise him. One man, being asked why he had so voted, answered: "Because I am tired of hearing Aristides called the just. There is a danger in goodness, for in the light of goodness evil stands condemned.*[3]

3. Noah was counted righteous (dikaios). Noah believed God and God counted his faith as righteousness. He "became heir of the righteousness *which is by faith*." As Matthew Henry says, Noah had faith in the *promised Seed*, the Savior whom God was someday going to send to earth.[4] There is nothing else upon earth that can cause God to count a man righteous but faith—faith in the *promised Seed*, the Savior of the world, even the Lord Jesus Christ.

"And he [Abraham] believed in the LORD; and he counted it to him for righteousness" (Ge.15:6).

"And by him all that believe are justified from all things, from which ye could not be justified by the law of Moses" (Ac.13:39).

"For all have sinned, and come short of the glory of God; being justified freely by his grace through the redemption that is in Christ Jesus" (Ro.3:23-24).

"For what saith the scripture? Abraham believed God, and it was counted unto him for righteousness" (Ro.4:3).

"Therefore being justified by faith, we have peace with God through our Lord Jesus Christ" (Ro.5:1).

"Much more then, being now justified by his blood, we shall be saved from wrath through him" (Ro.5:9).

"For he that is dead [counted dead, justified] is freed from sin" (Ro.6:7).

"Who shall lay any thing to the charge of God's elect? It is God that justifieth" (Ro.8:33).

"And such were some of you: but ye are washed, but ye are sanctified, but ye are justified in the name of the Lord Jesus, and by the Spirit of our God" (1 Co.6:11).

"Knowing that a man is not justified by the works of the law, but by the faith of Jesus Christ, even we have believed in Jesus Christ, that we might be justified by the faith of Christ, and not by the works of the law: for by the works of the law shall no flesh be justified" (Ga.2:16).

"Even as Abraham believed God, and it was accounted to him for righteousness" (Ga.3:6).

"Wherefore the law was our schoolmaster to bring us unto Christ, that we might be justified by faith" (Ga.3:24).

"And be found in him, not having mine own righteousness, which is of the law, but that which is through the faith of Christ, the righteousness which is of God by faith" (Ph.3:9).

---

2 *Matthew Henry's Commentary*, Vol.6, p.941.
3 William Barclay. *The Letter to the Hebrews*, p.160.
4 *Matthew Henry's Commentary*, Vol.6, p.941.

	F. Abraham's Faith (Part I): An Obedient, Hopeful Faith, 11:8-10

1. His faith: A faith that obeyed GodDS1
a. The great call of Abraham
b. The great faith of Abraham
  1) A decisive, obedient faith: Obeyed God's call
  2) A hopeful, obedient faith: Continued to follow God—as a pilgrim or foreigner upon earth
	8 By faith Abraham, when he was called to go out into a place which he should after receive for an inheritance, obeyed; and he went out, not knowing whither he went.
	9 By faith he sojourned in the land of promise, as *in* a strange country, dwelling in tabernacles with Isaac and Jacob, the heirs with him of the same promise:

2. His reward: The heavenly city that has an eternal foundation	10 For he looked for a city which hath foundations, whose builder and maker *is* God.

DIVISION IV

THE SUPREME AUTHOR OF FAITH: JESUS CHRIST, GOD'S SON, 10:19–11:40

F. Abraham's Faith (Part I): An Obedient, Hopeful Faith, 11:8-10

(11:8-10) **Introduction**: Abraham demonstrates one of the greatest examples of faith in the Bible. He believed against all odds and he endured in his faith. Abraham's faith was an obedient, believing faith—a faith that genuinely obeyed and believed God.

  1. His faith: a faith that obeyed God (vv.8-9).
  2. His reward: the heavenly city that has an eternal foundation (v.10).

1 (11:8-9) **Abraham—Faith**: Abraham's faith was a faith that obeyed and hoped in God. (See DEEPER STUDY # 1—Jn.4:22; notes—Ro.4:1-25; 9:7-13; Ga.3:6-7; 3:8-9; DEEPER STUDY # 1—3:8, 16.)

"Now the LORD had said unto Abram, Get thee out of thy country, and from thy kindred, and from thy father's house, unto a land that I will show thee: and I will make of thee a great nation, and I will bless thee, and make thy name great; and thou shalt be a blessing: and I will bless them that bless thee, and curse him that curseth thee: and in thee shall all families of the earth be blessed. So Abram departed, as the LORD had spoken unto him; and Lot went with him; and Abram was seventy and five years old when he departed out of Haran. And Abram took Sarai his wife, and Lot his brother's son, and all their substance that they had gathered, and the souls that they had gotten in Haran; and they went forth to go into the land of Canaan; and into the land of Canaan they came" (Ge.12:1-5; cp. Ge.11:26-32).

"And the LORD said unto Abram, after that Lot was separated from him, Lift up now thine eyes and look from the place where thou art northward, and southward, and eastward, and westward: for all the land which thou seest, to thee will I give it, and to thy seed for ever. And I will make thy seed as the dust of the earth: so that if a man can number the dust of the earth, then shall thy seed also be numbered. Arise, walk through the land in the length of it and in the breadth of it; for I will give it unto thee" (Ge.13:14-17).

"After these things the word of the LORD came unto Abram in a vision, saying, Fear not, Abram: I am thy shield, and thy exceeding great reward. And Abram said, Lord GOD, what wilt thou give me, seeing I go childless, and the steward of my house is this Eliezer of Damascus? And Abram said, Behold, to me thou hast given no seed: and, lo, one born in my house is mine heir. And, behold, the word of the LORD came unto him, saying, This shall not be thine heir; but he that shall come forth out of thine own bowels shall be thine heir. And he brought him forth abroad, and said, Look now toward heaven, and tell the stars, if thou be able to number them: and he said unto him, So shall thy seed be. And he believed in the LORD; and he counted it to him for righteousness. And he said unto him, I am the LORD that brought thee out of Ur of the Chaldees, to give thee this land to inherit it" (Ge.15:1-7).

"And when Abram was ninety years old and nine, the LORD apppeared to Abram, and said unto him, I am the Almighty God; walk before me, and be thou perfect. And I will make my covenant between me and thee, and will multiply thee exceedingly. And Abram fell on his face: and God talked with him, saying, as for me, behold, my covenant is with thee and thou shalt be a father of many nations. Neither shall thy name any more be called Abram, but thy name shall be Abraham; for a father of many nations have I made thee. And I will make thee exceeding fruitful, and I will make nations of thee, and kings shall come out of thee. And I will establish my covenant between me and thee and thy seed after thee in their generations for an everlasting covenant, to be a God unto thee, and to thy seed after thee. And I will give unto thee, and to thy seed after thee, the land wherein thou art a stranger, all the land of Canaan, for an everlasting possession; and I will be their God....And God said unto Abraham, As for Sarai thy wife, thou shalt not call her name Sarai, but Sarah shall her name be. And I will bless her, and give thee a son also of her: yea, I will bless her, and she shall be a mother of nations; kings of people shall be of her. Then Abraham fell upon his face, and laughed, and said in his heart, Shall a child be born unto him that is a hundred years old? and shall Sarah, that is ninety years old, bear? And Abraham said unto God, O that Ishmael might live before thee! And God said, Sarah thy wife shall bear thee a son indeed; and thou shalt call his name Isaac: and I will establish my covenant with him for an everlasting covenant, and with his seed after him" (Ge.17:1-7, 15-19).

"And the angel of the LORD called unto Abraham out of heaven the second time, and said, By myself have I sworn, saith the LORD, for because thou hast done this thing, and hast not withheld thy son, thine only son: that in blessing I will bless thee, and in multiplying I will multiply thy seed as the stars of the heaven, and as the sand which is upon the sea shore; and thy seed shall possess the gate of his enemies; and in thy seed shall all the nations of the earth be blessed; because thou hast obeyed my voice" (Ge.22:15-18).

"And he said, Men, brethren, and fathers, hearken; The God of glory appeared unto our father Abraham, when he was in Mesopotamia, before he dwelt in Charan, and said unto him, Get thee out of thy country, and from thy kindred, and come into the land which I shall show thee" (Ac.7:2-3).

"By faith Abraham, when he was called to go out into a place which he should after receive for an inheritance, obeyed; and he went out, not knowing whither he went. By faith he sojourned in the land of promise, as in a strange country, dwelling in tabernacles with Isaac and Jacob, the heirs with him of the same promise: for he looked for a city which hath foundations, whose builder and maker is God" (He.11:8-10).

Note two things about Abraham's faith.

1. God gave Abraham a great call. He called and challenged Abraham to be a witness to the other people of the world—a witness to the only living and true God. God challenged Abraham to separate himself from the world and to follow God—to leave his home, friends, employment, and his country. If Abraham would heed and obey God's call—if Abraham would obey God unquestionably—then God would do three wonderful things for Abraham.

⇒ God would cause a people to be born of his seed (Ge.12:1-5; Ro.4:17-18).
⇒ God would bless all nations through his seed (Ge.12:2; Ro.4:17-18; Ga.3:8, 16).
⇒ God would give him a promised land, the land of Canaan (Ge.12:1; Ro.4:13; He.11:8-10, 13-16).

"For as many as are led by the Spirit of God, they are the sons of God. For ye have not received the spirit of bondage again to fear; but ye have received the Spirit of adoption, whereby we cry, Abba, Father. The Spirit itself beareth witness with our spirit, that we are the children of God: and if children, then heirs; heirs of God, and joint-heirs with Christ; if so be that we suffer with him, that we may be also glorified together" (Ro.8:14-17).

"Wherefore come out from among them, and be ye separate, saith the Lord, and touch not the unclean thing; and I will receive you, and will be a Father unto you, and ye shall be my sons and daughters, saith the Lord Almighty" (2 Co.6:17-18).

"Who will have all men to be saved, and to come unto the knowledge of the truth" (1 Ti.2:4).

2. Abraham obeyed God; he believed God. Note exactly the kind of faith he had.

a. He had a *decisive, obedient faith*. He obeyed, and he went out not knowing where he went. When God called, he acted immediately. He did not hesitate, argue, question, equivocate, or waver back and forth. He obeyed. As soon as he heard the call of God, he got up and followed God: he acted decisively.

Note a significant fact about following God. Abraham did not know where he was going. He did not know where following God would lead him. He just believed the promises of God; therefore, he acted upon his belief. He believed; therefore, he obeyed.

Thought 1. A person who truly believes God obeys God. There is no such thing as belief without obedience, not genuine belief.

Thought 2. No person knows where his faith will lead him, but he is not to fear following God. God is good and He has only good things in store for any true follower of His. If we draw back and do not believe and follow God, then we shall miss out on the promises of God.

b. He had a hopeful, obedient faith. Note that Abraham never received the inheritance of the promised land, and he never saw a nation of people born of his seed. In fact, Abraham never even owned a piece of land upon which he could settle and live. He was only a *sojourner*, a wanderer from place to place in a strange country. He even lived to a ripe old age, seeing both his son and grandson born, and he witnessed them become the heirs of promise. But even they were heirs of the promise, not the inheritors of the land. He never even saw them receive one parcel of land. But despite it all—despite what appeared to be all kinds of odds against the promises of God ever being fulfilled—Abraham still believed in God. He still believed in the hope God had given him. He believed it so strongly that he even taught *the same promises* to his son Isaac and to his grandson Jacob.

"Not every one that saith unto me, Lord, Lord, shall enter into the kingdom of heaven; but he that doeth the will of my Father which is in heaven" (Mt.7:21).

"Therefore whosoever heareth these sayings of mine, and doeth them, I will liken him unto a wise man, which built his house upon a rock: and the rain descended, and the floods came, and the winds blew, and beat upon that house; and it fell not: for it was founded upon a rock" (Mt.7:24-25).

"And being made perfect, he became the author of eternal salvation unto all them that obey him" (He.5:9).

"Blessed are they that do his commandments, that they may have right to the tree of life, and may enter in through the gates into the city" (Re.22:14).

DEEPER STUDY # 1

(11:8-9) **Abraham—Faith**: What did Abraham believe? (See DEEPER STUDY # 1—Ro.4:1-25; note—9:7-13; DEEPER STUDY # 1—Ga.3:8, 16.)

1. He believed that God would create a nation through his seed (Ge.12:2-5; Ro.4:17-18).
2. He believed that God would give a child against all odds (Ge.15:1-6; Ro.4:18-22; He.11:11-12).
3. He believed in the eternal city (He.11:8-10, 13-16).
4. He believed in God's power to raise the dead (He.11:17-19).

---

2 (11:10) **Abraham—Faith**: Abraham's reward was the great city that had foundations, whose builder and maker is God. The great heavenly city was his hope. This verse plainly says that Abraham's faith was the faith that looked beyond this world to heaven. This is a phenomenal declaration: that Abraham believed in the heavenly city of God, in a future life—a life that would put him in the presence of God forever and ever. Yet, this is exactly what is declared in this Scripture by the Holy Spirit through the writer to the Hebrews. Paul even says that the promise made to Abraham was "that he should be the heir of the world" (Ro.4:13). This refers, of course, to the new heavens and earth (see 2 Pe.3:10-13; Re.21:1f).

The point to see is the great faith of Abraham. He believed that God was going to give him the land of Canaan which was a type or symbol of the great land of heaven, the great city whose builder is God.

"For the promise, that he should be their heir of the world, was not to Abraham, or to his seed, through the law, but through the righteousness of faith" (Ro.4:13).

"For he looked for a city which hath foundations, whose builder and maker is God" (He.11:10).

"But now they desire a better country, that is, an heavenly: wherefore God is not ashamed to be called their God: for he hath prepared for them a city" (He.11:16).

"But ye are come unto mount Sion, and unto the city of the living God, the heavenly Jerusalem, and to an innumerable company of angels" (He.12:22).

"For here have we no continuing city, but we seek one to come" (He.13:14).

"But the day of the Lord will come as a thief in the night; in the which the heavens shall pass away with a great noise, and the elements shall melt with fervent heat, the earth also and the works that are therein shall be burned. Seeing then that all these things shall be dissolved, what manner of persons ought ye to be in all holy conversation and godliness, looking for and hasting unto the coming of the day of God, wherein the heavens being on fire shall be dissolved, and the elements shall melt with fervent heat?" (2 Pe.3:10-13).

"And I saw a new heaven and a new earth: for the first heaven and the first earth were passed away; and there was no more sea. And I John saw the holy city, new Jerusalem, coming down from God out of heaven, prepared as a bride adorned for her husband. And I heard a great voice out of heaven saying, Behold, the tabernacle of God is with men, and he will dwell with them, and they shall be his people, and God himself shall be with them, and be their God. And God shall wipe away all tears from their eyes; and there shall be no more death, neither sorrow, nor crying, neither shall there be any more pain: for the former things are passed away" (Re.21:1-4).

"And he carried me away in the spirit to a great and high mountain, and showed me that great city, the holy Jerusalem, descending out of heaven from God" (Re.21:10).

"Blessed are they that do his commandments, that they may have right to the tree of life, and may enter in through the gates into the city" (Re.22:14).

"And if any man shall take away from the words of the book of this prophecy, God shall take away his part out of the book of life, and out of the holy city, and from the things which are written in this book" (Re.22:19).

	G. Sarah's Faith: An Impossible Faith, 11:11-12
1. Her faith: A faith that believed the impossible	11 Through faith also Sara herself received strength to conceive seed, and was delivered of a child when she was past age, because she judged him faithful who had promised.
2. Her reward: The promised son & a nation of believing descendants	12 Therefore sprang there even of one, and him as good as dead, *so many* as the stars of the sky in multitude, and as the sand which is by the sea shore innumerable.

DIVISION IV

THE SUPREME AUTHOR OF FAITH: JESUS CHRIST, GOD'S SON, 10:19–11:40

G. Sarah's Faith: An Impossible Faith, 11:11-12

(11:11-12) **Introduction**: Sarah is a dynamic example of what it is to believe the impossible. She believed the impossible; therefore, she saw God do the impossible.

    1. Her faith: a faith that believed the impossible (v.11).
    2. Her reward: the promised son and a nation of believing descendants (v.12).

[1]   (11:11) **Sarah—Faith**: Sarah's faith was a faith that believed the impossible.

       "And they said unto him, Where is Sarah thy wife? And he said, Behold, in the tent. And he said, I will certainly return unto thee according to the time of life; and, lo, Sarah heard it in the tent door, which was behind him. Now Abraham and Sarah were old and well stricken in age; and it ceased to be with Sarah after the manner of women. Therefore Sarah laughed within herself, saying, After I am waxed old shall I have pleasure, my lord being old also? And the LORD said unto Abraham, Wherefore did Sarah laugh, saying, Shall I of a surety bear a child, which am old? Is any thing too hard for the LORD? At the time appointed I will return unto thee, according to the time of life, and Sarah shall have a son. Then Sarah denied, saying, I laughed not; for she was afraid. And he said, Nay; but thou didst laugh" (Ge.18:9-15; cp. Ge.17:15-22).

       "And the LORD visited Sarah as he had said, and the LORD did unto Sarah as he had spoken. For Sarah conceived, and bare Abraham a son in his old age, at the set time of which God had spoken to him. And Abraham called the name of his son that was born unto him, whom Sarah bare to him, Isaac. And Abraham circumcised his son Isaac being eight days old, as God had commanded him. And Abraham was a hundred years old, when his son Isaac was born unto him" (Ge.21:1-5).

       "Who against hope believed in hope, that he [Abraham] might become the father of many nations, according to that which was spoken, So shall thy seed be. And being not weak in faith, he considered not his own body now dead, when he was about an hundred years old, neither yet the deadness of Sarah's womb: he staggered not at the promise of God through unbelief; but was strong in faith, giving glory to God; and being fully persuaded that, what he had promised he was able also to perform" (Ro.4:18-21).

       "Through faith also Sarah herself received strength to conceive seed, and was delivered of a child when she was past age [90 years old], because she judged him faithful who had promised. Therefore sprang there even of one, and him as good as dead, so many as the stars of the sky in multitude, and as the sand which is by the sea shore innumerable" (He.11:11-12).

    Note two significant facts.

    1. Sarah had difficulty believing God at first. When she first heard the promise of God she doubted the promise. In the Genesis account the Lord appeared and talked with Abraham right outside the door of Abraham's tent. Sarah hid in the tent with her ear up close so she could hear the conversation. When she overheard the Lord promise a child to Abraham, Sarah laughed, for she and Abraham were well past child-bearing age (see Ge.18:12). They were both humanly sterile.

    Thought 1. The promises of God do sound unbelievable. Just think how corrupt, sinful, evil, savage, violent, and doomed to death the human race is. Any daily news media is filled with illustrations of man's corruption. Yet God loves the world, loves it so much that He has promised "the seed" of the Savior to the world. Just think how unbelievable this sounds.

⇒ God has promised a Savior who will bear the sins of man for him and present him to God as righteous.
⇒ God has promised a Savior who will save man from the corruption and death of the world, a Savior who can give man life—eternal life in a new heavens and earth.

2. Sarah considered the matter: who it was that was making the promise, God Himself, the Sovereign Majesty of the universe. When Sarah considered this, the change in her was dramatic: if it was God who was making the promise, then God could be *counted* (*judged*) faithful. God always fulfills His promises. God could do it no matter how difficult the situation was...

- despite the human impossibility
- despite the fact that all reason spoke against it
- despite the fact that nature had to be overridden

Sarah believed God. She switched from unbelief to belief. She trusted the promise of God. Therefore, she bore a child at the age of ninety. It was a miraculous birth, but God had promised and He fulfilled His promise.

Thought 1. God cannot lie; He cannot deceive people. Therefore, the promises of God—every single one of them—shall be fulfilled. But note: the promise of the *seed*, that is, of the Savior, applies only to those who believe.

"But Jesus beheld them, and said unto them, With men this is impossible; but with God all things are possible" (Mt.19:26).
"Jesus said unto him, If thou canst believe, all things are possible to him that believeth" (Mk.9:23).
"And he said, Abba, Father, all things are possible unto thee; take away this cup from me: nevertheless not what I will, but what thou wilt" (Mk.14:36).
"For with God nothing shall be impossible" (Lu.1:37).
"I know that thou canst do every thing, and that no thought can be withholden from thee" (Jb.42:2).
"Oh how great is thy goodness, which thou hast laid up for them that fear thee; which thou hast wrought for them that trust in thee before the sons of men!" (Ps.31:19).
"Commit thy way unto the LORD; trust also in him; and he shall bring it to pass" (Ps.37:5).
"God hath spoken once; twice have I heard this; that power belongeth unto God" (Ps.62:11).
"Trust in the LORD with all thine heart; and lean not unto thine own understanding" (Pr.3:5).
"Trust ye in the LORD for ever: for in the LORD JEHOVAH is everlasting strength" (Is.26:4).

2 (11:12) **Sarah—Faith**: Sarah's faith was rewarded. She received the promised son and nation through her seed. This refers to two rewards:
⇒ the gift of *the seed Isaac* and of the nation of Israel.
⇒ the gift of *the seed Christ* and of the nation of believers, of the new creation of *born again* men and women, those who shall be citizens of God's new heavens and earth (see DEEPER STUDY # 1—Ga.3:8, notes—Ga.3:16; Ep.2:11-18; 2:14-15; 3:16; 4:17-19. See DEEPER STUDY # 1—Jn.4:22; DEEPER STUDY # 1—Ro.4:1-25.)

Sarah believed the impossible, and God rewarded her faith: she *received* the impossible. Look at Israel. Israel exists today because Sarah believed the impossible promise of God. Look at the believers around the world, those who profess to be born again by the sacrifice of Jesus Christ for their sins. They exist today because Sarah believed the impossible promise of God.

"Jesus answered and said unto him, Verily, verily, I say unto thee, Except a man be born again, he cannot see the kingdom of God....Jesus answered, Verily, verily, I say unto thee, Except a man be born of water and of the Spirit, he cannot enter into the kingdom of God. That which is born of the flesh is flesh; and that which is born of the Spirit is spirit. Marvel not that I said unto thee, Ye must be born again" (Jn.3:3, 5-7).
"Therefore if any man be in Christ, he is a new creature: old things are passed away; behold, all things are become new" (2 Co.5:17).
"Being born again, not of corruptible seed, but of incorruptible, by the word of God, which liveth and abideth for ever" (1 Pe.1:23).
"Whosoever believeth that Jesus is the Christ is born of God: and every one that loveth him that begat loveth him also that is begotten [born again] of him" (1 Jn.5:1).
"But without faith it is impossible to please him: for he that cometh to God must believe that he is, and that he is a rewarder of them that diligently seek him" (He.11:6).
"For he is not a Jew, which is one outwardly; neither is that circumcision, which is outward in the flesh: but he is a Jew, which is one inwardly; and circumcision is that of the heart, in the spirit, and not in the letter; whose praise is not of men, but of God" (Ro.2:28-29).
"And if ye be Christ's, then are ye Abraham's seed, and heirs according to the promise" (Ga.3:29).

| 1. Their faith: A faith that endured—that forever sought an unseen, heavenly country
   a. A visionary faith: They saw
   b. A growing faith: They saw & welcomed the promises of God
   c. A working faith: They sought & declared that they were | **H. The Patriarch's Faith: A Pilgrim's Faith, 11:13-16**

 13 These all died in faith, not having received the promises, but having seen them afar off, and were persuaded of *them,* and embraced *them,* and confessed that they were strangers and pilgrims on the earth.
 14 For they that say such things declare plainly that | they seek a country.
 15 And truly, if they had been mindful of that *country* from whence they came out, they might have had opportunity to have returned.
 16 But now they desire a better *country,* that is, an heavenly: wherefore God is not ashamed to be called their God: for he hath prepared for them a city. | seeking a country of their own
   d. An enduring faith: They did not return

 2. Their reward
   a. God's approval
   b. God's heavenly city |

DIVISION IV

THE SUPREME AUTHOR OF FAITH: JESUS CHRIST, GOD'S SON, 10:19–11:40

H. The Patriarch's Faith: A Pilgrim's Faith, 11:13-16

(11:13-16) **Introduction**: believers are only strangers and pilgrims on earth. They are only passing through this earth and this life which is ever so brief and corrupt. They are heirs and citizens of heaven. This passage is a picture of the great faith of believers, the faith of God's pilgrims upon earth.

1. Their faith: A faith that endured—that forever sought an unseen, heavenly country (vv.13-15).
2. Their reward (v.16).

[1] (11:13-15) **Patriarchs—Faith—Pilgrimage**: the patriarch's faith was a faith that endured, that forever sought an unseen, heavenly country. The word patriarch refers to Abraham, Isaac, Jacob, and other ancient men who had great faith in God and His promises. The point to see is this: these all died believing what God had promised and not a single one of them ever received the promise on earth. If they were to receive them, they had to accept them by faith. Believing them—hoping in them—was the only way they could possess them. Note four points.

1. Their faith was a *visionary faith*. They saw the promises of God afar off, not by sight but in their hearts and minds. What was the promise? It was the promise…
   - of a country (v.14)
   - of a better country, a heavenly world (v.16). Christ Jesus even said that Abraham saw His day and rejoiced in the hope of it (see Jn.8:56)

Thought 1. How much more we can see and understand the promises of God. Christ has already come once. To believe that He shall return is much easier than Abraham believing that He was coming the first time. Abraham had no precedent, whereas we do.

2. Their faith was a *growing faith*.
   ⇒ They saw the promise of God and were thankful to God for the privilege of seeing it.
   ⇒ They were persuaded of the promises of God. They believed that the promises were true, that there was a promised land and that God was going to give it to them. They believed in God and that what God promised He was going to fulfill.
   ⇒ They embraced (aspasamenoi) the promises. The word means to greet and welcome. They were ever so thankful and appreciative to God for such a glorious hope as the promised land. They rejoiced and loved the promise, setting their eyes upon it and not looking away.
   ⇒ They confessed that they were only strangers and pilgrims upon earth, just passing through until they could inherit the glorious hope of the promised land. They confessed the glorious hope to all; they bore testimony and witness and did so unashamedly that God had given them the hope of the promised land.

3. Their faith was a *working faith*. They actively sought after the promised land and declared the fact to all.
   ⇒ They did not just sit back and talk about the promised land, thinking that God would take them to it when it was time.
   ⇒ They did no go on about their lives upon this earth ignoring the promised land, thinking that they were good enough and God would never reject them from inheriting it.

The early believers actively sought after the promised land. They got up and went looking for it, leaving the world and its possessions behind. By their separation from the world and seeking after God's promises, they declared plainly that they were men and women of true faith.

4. Their faith was an *enduring faith*. They never returned to the country they had left. They had separated from the world and began a search for the promised land of God and they stayed on the search.

Simply stated, they kept their mind and thoughts upon the promised land.

⇒ They did not harbor the thoughts of the old world's pleasures and desires, possessions and indulgences, feelings and comforts.

⇒ They did not return to the old world when they had the chance.

⇒ The patriarchs endured to the end. In fact, they went to their grave believing in the great hope of God for the promised land.

"And being fully persuaded that, what he had promised, he was able also to perform" (Ro.4:21).

"For I am persuaded, that neither death, nor life, nor angels, nor principalities, nor powers, nor things present, nor things to come, nor height, nor depth, nor any other creature, shall be able to separate us from the love of God, which is in Christ Jesus our Lord" (Ro.8:38-39).

"For the which cause I also suffer these things: nevertheless I am not ashamed: for I know whom I have believed, and am persuaded that he is able to keep that which I have committed unto him against that day" (2 Ti.1:12).

"For our conversation [citizenship] is in heaven; from whence also we look for the Saviour, the Lord Jesus Christ: who shall change our vile body, that it may be fashioned like unto his glorious body, according to the working whereby he is able even to subdue all things unto himself" (Ph.3:20-21).

"These all died in faith, not having received the promises, but having seen them afar off, and were persuaded of them, and embraced them, and confessed that they were strangers and pilgrims on the earth" (He.11:13).

"For here have we no continuing city, but we seek one to come" (He.13:14).

"For we are strangers before thee, and sojourners, as were all our fathers: our days on the earth are as a shadow, and there is none abiding" (1 Chr.29:15).

"Hear my prayer, O LORD, and give ear unto my cry; hold not thy peace at my tears: for I am a stranger with thee, and a sojourner, as all my fathers were" (Ps.39:12).

"I am a stranger in the earth: hide not thy commandments from me" (Ps.119:19).

---

2 (11:16) **Faith—Reward**: the reward of the patriarchs. Their reward was twofold.

1. They received God's approval. God is not ashamed to be called their God. Note the present tense: they are still living, even today. And so is God. God is acting now; it is today that He is unashamed. He is the God of Abraham, Isaac, and Jacob today, and He is not ashamed to be called their God. Just imagine! These great patriarchs have been alive and living in God's presence for thousands of years (see Mt.22:32; Mk.12:26; Lu.20:37). God loves and commits Himself to all who believe Him and His promises. He is not ashamed and never will be ashamed of those who confess that they seek Him and the country He has promised.

"For God so loved the world, that he gave his only begotten Son, that whosoever believeth in him should not perish, but have everlasting life" (Jn.3:16).

"For whether we live, we live unto the Lord; and whether we die, we die unto the Lord: whether we live therefore, or die, we are the Lord's" (Ro.14:8).

"For to me to live is Christ, and to die is gain" (Ph.1:21).

"These all died in faith, not having received the promises, but having seen them afar off, and were persuaded of them, and embraced them, and confessed that they were strangers and pilgrims on the earth" (He.11:13).

"And I heard a voice from heaven saying unto me, Write, Blessed are the dead which die in the Lord from henceforth: Yea, saith the Spirit, that they may rest from their labours; and their works do follow them" (Re.14:13).

"But in every nation he that feareth him, and worketh righteousness, is accepted with him" (Ac.10:35).

"Therefore we are always confident, knowing that, whilst we are at home in the body, we are absent from the Lord: (For we walk by faith, not by sight:) we are confident, I say, and willing rather to be absent from the body, and to be present with the Lord. Wherefore we labour, that, whether present or absent, we may be accepted of him. For we must all appear before the judgment seat of Christ; that every one may receive the things done in his body, according to that he hath done, whether it be good or bad" (2 Co.5:6-10).

"Wherefore come out from among them, and be ye separate, saith the Lord, and touch not the unclean thing; and I will receive you, and will be a Father unto you, and ye shall be my sons and daughters, saith the Lord Almighty" (2 Co.6:17-18).

"To the praise of the glory of his grace, wherein he hath made us accepted in the beloved. In whom we have redemption through his blood, the forgiveness of sins, according to the riches of his grace" (Ep.1:6-7).

"Now therefore, if ye will obey my voice indeed, and keep my covenant, then ye shall be a peculiar treasure unto me above all people: for all the earth is mine" (Ex.19:5).

2. They received the promised land. God prepared a city for them, a heavenly city that will last forever and ever.

"For the promise, that he should be the heir of the world, was not to Abraham, or to his seed, through the law, but through the righteousness of faith" (Ro.4:13).

"For he looked for a city which hath foundations, whose builder and maker is God" (He.11:10).

"But now they desire a better country, that is, an heavenly: wherefore God is not ashamed to be called their God: for he hath prepared for them a city" (He.11:16).

"But ye are come unto mount Sion, and unto the city of the living God, the heavenly Jerusalem, and to an innumerable company of angels" (He.12:22).

"For here have we no continuing city, but we seek one to come" (He.13:14).

"But the day of the Lord will come as a thief in the night; in the which the heavens shall pass away with a great noise, and the elements shall melt with fervent heat, the earth also and the works that are therein shall be burned. Seeing then that all these things shall be dissolved, what manner of persons ought ye to be in all holy conversation and godlinesss, looking for and hasting unto the coming of the day of God, wherein the heavens being on fire shall be dissolved, and the elements shall melt with fervent heat?" (2 Pe.3:10-13).

"And I saw a new heaven and a new earth: for the first heaven and the first earth were passed away; and there was no more sea. And I John saw the holy city, new Jerusalem, coming down from God out of heaven, prepared as a bride adorned for her husband. And I heard a great voice out of heaven saying, Behold, the tabernacle of God is with men, and he will dwell with them, and they shall be his people, and God himself shall be with them, and be their God. And God shall wipe away all tears from their eyes; and there shall be no more death, neither sorrow, nor crying, neither shall there be any more pain: for the former things are passed away" (Re.21:1-4).

"And he carried me away in the spirit to a great and high mountain, and showed me that great city, the holy Jerusalem, descending out of heaven from God" (Re.21:10).

"Blessed are they that do his commandments, that they may have right to the tree of life, and may enter in through the gates into the city" (Re.22:14).

"And if any man shall take away from the words of the book of this prophecy, God shall take away his part out of the book of life, and out of the holy city, and from the things which are written in this book" (Re.22:19).

	I. Abraham's Faith (Part II): A Sacrificial Faith, 11:17-19
1. His faith: A faith that obeyed God regardless of cost a. God's unbelievable command: To sacrifice Isaac, his one & only son	17 By faith Abraham, when he was tried, offered up Isaac: and he that had received the promises offered up his only begotten *son,* 18 Of whom it was said, That in Isaac shall thy seed be called:
b. Abraham's great faith: Counted God as trustworthy **2. His reward: Deliverance**	19 Accounting that God *was* able to raise *him* up, even from the dead; from whence also he received him in a figure.

DIVISION IV

THE SUPREME AUTHOR OF FAITH: JESUS CHRIST, GOD'S SON, 10:19–11:40

I.   Abraham's Faith (Part II): A Sacrificial Faith, 11:17-19

(11:17-19) **Introduction**: this act of Abraham is the supreme act of faith. This is the picture of sacrificial faith, the faith which God demands of every man, the faith without which a person shall never inherit the promises of God.

1. His faith: a faith that obeyed God regardless of cost (vv.17-19).
2. His reward: deliverance (v.19).

1 (11:17-19) **Abraham—Faith**: Abraham's faith was a faith that obeyed God regardless of cost. This demand made upon Abraham was the supreme act of faith (see Ge.22:1-18).

"And it came to pass after these things, that God did tempt Abraham, and said unto him, Abraham: and he said, Behold, here I am. And he said, Take now thy son, thine only son Isaac, whom thou lovest, and get thee into the land of Moriah; and offer him there for a burnt offering upon one of the mountains which I will tell thee of. And Abraham rose up early in the morning, and saddled his ass, and took two of his young men with him, and Isaac his son, and clave the wood for the burnt offering, and rose up, and went unto the place of which God had told him....And they came to the place which God had told him of; and Abraham built an altar there, and laid the wood in order, and bound Isaac his son, and laid him on the altar upon the wood. And Abraham stretched forth his hand, and took the knife to slay his son. And the angel of the LORD called unto him out of heaven, and said, Abraham, Abraham: and he said, Here am I. And he said, Lay not thine hand upon the lad, neither do thou any thing unto him: for now I know that thou fearest God, seeing thou hast not withheld thy son, thine only son from me....And the angel of the LORD called unto Abraham out of heaven the second time, and said, By myself have I sworn, saith the LORD, for because thou hast done this thing, and hast not withheld thy son, thine only son: that in blessing I will bless thee, and in multiplying I will multiply thy seed as the stars of the heaven, and as the sand which is upon the sea shore; and thy seed shall possess the gate of his enemies; and in thy seed shall all the nations of the earth be blessed; because thou hast obeyed my voice" (Ge.22:1-3, 9-12, 15-18).

"By faith Abraham, when he was tried, offered up Isaac: and he that had received the promises offered up his only begotten son, of whom it was said, That in Isaac shall thy seed be called: accounting that God was able to raise him up, even from the dead; from whence also he received him in a figure" (He.11:17-19).

Note two significant points.

1. God's unbelievable command. God commanded Abraham to take Isaac and to offer him up as a sacrifice to Him. To say the least this was a most unusual command, that is, God commanding that a human sacrifice be made to Him. William Barclay has a comment about this fact that states it well:

To some extent this story has fallen into disrepute nowadays. It does not appear in syllabuses of religious education because it is held to teach a view of God that can no longer be accepted. Or, failing that, it is held to teach that the point of the story is that it was in this way that Abraham learned that God did not desire human sacrifice. There were days when men considered it a sacred duty to offer up their first-born sons to God, before they learned that God would never desire a sacrifice like that. No doubt that is true; but if we want to see this story at its greatest, and if we want to see it as the writer to the Hebrews saw it, we must take it at its face value. It was the response of a man who was asked to offer to God his own son.[1]

What was God doing? We can say several things.

    a. God was testing the faith of Abraham in the most supreme way possible. We must always remember that God had made the supreme promises to Abraham:

    ⇒ The supreme promise of the *seed* of the Savior, of God's very own Son.

    ⇒ The supreme hope of the promised land and of dwelling in the very presence of God Himself. And the inheritance was to be for eternity.

    ⇒ The supreme promise of an unlimited nation of people, a people that would endure forever.

    ⇒ The supreme promise of being a blessing to all the nations of the world, an eternal blessing.

A man who had received the supreme promises of God had to be tested in the most supreme way possible. And, no doubt, in light of what God demanded of Abraham, the most supreme way in Abraham's day and time was to demand that Abraham sacrifice his only son. Remember how difficult this was for Abraham. He loved Isaac dearly, for Isaac was not only his only son, but Abraham's whole life—his past and future were wrapped up in Isaac. Abraham had lived for Isaac, his only son. All the promises of God to him were wrapped up in Isaac. What an unbelievable faith Abraham had!

    b. God was using the offering of Isaac as a sacrifice to symbolize the offering up of God's only Son as the sacrifice for man's sins. God was also using Abraham's faith that God could raise up the dead to proclaim that man must believe *that God can raise the dead.* God is going to; therefore, man must believe it in order to be resurrected.

> **"The next day John seeth Jesus coming unto him, and saith, Behold the Lamb of God, which taketh away the sin of the world" (Jn.1:29).**
> **"Greater love hath no man than this, that a man lay down his life for his friends" (Jn.15:13).**
> **"For when we were yet without strength, in due time Christ died for the ungodly" (Ro.5:6).**
> **"For I delivered unto you first of all that which I also received, how that Christ died for our sins according to the scriptures; and that he was buried, and that he rose again the third day according to the scriptures: and that he was seen of Cephas, then of the twelve" (1 Co.15:3-5).**
> **"Who gave himself for our sins, that he might deliver us from this present evil world, according to the will of God and our Father" (Ga.1:4).**
> **"And walk in love, as Christ also hath loved us, and hath given himself for us an offering and a sacrifice to God for a sweetsmelling savour" (Ep.5:2).**
> **"Who gave himself for us, that he might redeem us from all iniquity, and purify unto himself a peculiar people, zealous of good works" (Tit.2:14).**
> **"Forasmuch as ye know that ye were not redeemed with corruptible things, as silver and gold, from your vain conversation [behavior] received by tradition from your fathers; but with the precious blood of Christ, as of a lamb without blemish and without spot" (1 Pe.1:18-19).**
> **"Hereby perceive we the love of God, because he laid down his life for us: and we ought to lay down our lives for the brethren" (1 Jn.3:16).**
> **"And from Jesus Christ, who is the faithful witness, and the first begotten of the dead, and the prince of the kings of the earth. Unto him that loved us, and washed us from our sins in his own blood" (Re.1:5).**

    c. God was also teaching that man must trust God to the ultimate degree. Man must be willing to sacrifice the thing he loves the most and holds dearest to his heart. He must love God supremely, love God and His promises above all else. God will not accept second best and divided loyalty. He demands to be first in the life of every person. A person either puts Him first or else he is unacceptable to God and misses out on the promises of God.

  2. Abraham's great faith was the ultimate faith. Abraham considered and thought through the demand of God. He knew God was God; therefore...

- he knew that God gave no foolish commands
- he knew that God could stop him anywhere along the road to the mountain where he was to sacrifice Isaac, and if not, then God could raise Isaac from the dead
- he knew that God never broke His promises and that God could not fulfill His promises without Isaac

Abraham counted God trustworthy—true and faithful to His promise. Therefore, he stepped out to follow God supremely.

Thought 1. Note how Abraham loved God supremely. Abraham put God above all, even above the person whom he loved the most, his own dear son.

> **"But Jesus beheld them, and said unto them, With men this is impossible; but with God all things are possible" (Mt.19:26).**
> **"Jesus said unto him, If thou canst believe, all things are possible to him that believeth" (Mk.9:23).**
> **"For with God nothing shall be impossible" (Lu.1:37).**

---

[1] William Barclay. *The Letter to the Hebrews*, p.171.

"Verily, verily, I say unto you, He that heareth my word, and believeth on him that sent me, hath everlasting life, and shall not come into condemnation; but is passed from death unto life" (Jn.5:24).

"Even as Abraham believed God, and it was accounted to him for righteousness" (Ga.3:6).

"But without faith it is impossible to please him: for he that cometh to God must believe that he is, and that he is a rewarder of them that diligently seek him" (He.11:6).

"Even so faith, if it hath not works, is dead, being alone" (Js.2:17).

"God hath spoken once; twice have I heard this; that power belongeth unto God" (Ps.62:11).

"But our God is in the heavens: he hath done whatsoever he hath pleased" (Ps.115:3).

---

2 (11:19) **Abraham—Faith—Reward**: Abraham's reward was deliverance, the deliverance of his son from the dead. The idea is this: Isaac was as good as dead in Abraham's mind. Abraham was totally committed to sacrifice Isaac; he was totally committed to love God and His Word supremely. That was enough for God. God had His answer. Abraham believed God and loved Him above the most dear thing on earth. Therefore, when God stopped the judgment upon Isaac, it was like a resurrection from the dead. The point to us is the three lessons given in the former note:

⇒ We must trust God supremely, love and trust Him above everyone and all else.

⇒ We must believe God even when we cannot understand the ways and commands of God.

⇒ We must trust the sacrifice of God's own dear Son for our sins and trust His resurrection as the assurance of our being resurrected and living forever with God.

"That whosoever believeth in him should not perish, but have eternal life. For God so loved the world, that he gave his only begotten Son, that whosoever believeth in him should not perish, but have everlasting life" (Jn.3:15-16).

"Verily, verily, I say unto you, He that heareth my word, and believeth on him that sent me, hath everlasting life, and shall not come into condemnation; but is passed from death unto life. Verily, verily, I say unto you, The hour is coming, and now is, when the dead shall hear the voice of the Son of God: and they that hear shall live" (Jn.5:24-25).

"And this is the will of him that sent me, that every one which seeth the Son, and believeth on him, may have everlasting life: and I will raise him up at the last day" (Jn.6:40).

"Verily, verily, I say unto you, If a man keep my saying, he shall never see death" (Jn.8:51).

"Jesus said unto her, I am the resurrection, and the life: he that believeth in me, though he were dead, yet shall he live" (Jn.11:25).

"For this corruptible must put on incorruption, and this mortal must put on immortality. So when this corruptible shall have put on incorruption, and this mortal shall have put on immortality, then shall be brought to pass the saying that is written, Death is swallowed up in victory" (1 Co.15:53-54).

"For we know that if our earthly house of this tabernacle were dissolved, we have a building of God, an house not made with hands, eternal in the heavens" (2 Co.5:1).

"For the Lord himself shall descend from heaven with a shout, with the voice of the archangel, and with the trump of God: and the dead in Christ shall rise first: then we which are alive and remain shall be caught up together with them in the clouds, to meet the Lord in the air: and so shall we ever be with the Lord. Wherefore comfort one another with these words" (1 Th.4:16-18).

"But is now made manifest by the appearing of our Saviour Jesus Christ, who hath abolished death, and hath brought life and immortality to light through the gospel" (2 Ti.1:10).

"But God will redeem my soul from the power of the grave: for he shall receive me" (Ps.49:15).

"Thou, which hast showed me great and sore troubles, shalt quicken me again, and shalt bring me up again from the depths of the earth" (Ps.71:20).

"I will ransom them from the power of the grave; I will redeem them from death: O death, I will be thy plagues; O grave, I will be thy destruction: repentance shall be hid from mine eyes" (Ho.13:14).

	J. Isaac's Faith: A Strong, Futuristic Faith, 11:20
1. A faith that believed in God 2. A faith that believed in the future	20 By faith Isaac blessed Jacob and Esau concerning things to come.

DIVISION IV

THE SUPREME AUTHOR OF FAITH: JESUS CHRIST, GOD'S SON, 10:19–11:40

J.   Isaac's Faith: A Strong, Futuristic Faith, 11:20

(11:20) **Introduction**: Isaac is the prime example of a person who believes the promises of God, but needs to repent before he can receive them. Isaac is an example of the person who believes in the things to come despite sin.

1. A faith that believed in God (v.20).
2. A faith that believed in the future (v.20).

1 (11:20) **Isaac—Faith**: Isaac's faith was a faith that believed in the things to come despite sin (Ge.27:1-40). Isaac believed that God would fulfill His promises through his sons, fulfill His promises despite the selfishness and conniving deception of his sons.

Jacob was the younger son who stuck closer to his mother. He was somewhat of a homebody. Esau was Isaac's older son, a true outdoorsman just like Isaac. Therefore, Isaac preferred Esau. He wanted Esau to receive the greater blessing of God, in particular he wanted Esau to be *the seed* through whom God would fulfill His promise of a promised land and of a nation of people.

Isaac was aged and blind when he was ready to pass the blessing on to his sons. Now note several facts.

⇒   God had told Isaac and his wife, Rebekah, that Jacob was to be the one who was to receive the blessing; the older son was to serve the younger.

> **"And the LORD said unto her, Two nations are in thy womb, and two manner of people shall be separated from thy bowels; and the one people shall be stronger than the other people; and the elder shall serve the younger" (Ge.25:23).**

⇒   Isaac was reluctant to obey God. In fact, he did not want to obey God; he preferred Esau. When it came time to pass the blessings of God's promise on to his son, Isaac planned to ignore God's will and bless Esau.

> **"And it came to pass, that when Isaac was old, and his eyes were dim, so that he could not see, he called Esau his eldest son, and said unto him, My son: and he said unto him, Behold, here am I. And he said, Behold now, I am old, I know not the day of my death: now therefore take, I pray thee, thy weapons, thy quiver and thy bow, and go out to the field, and take me some venison; and make me savory meat, such as I love, and bring it to me, that I may eat; that my soul may bless thee before I die" (Ge.27:1-4).**

⇒   Rebekah overheard Isaac's plans to ignore and bypass God's will. Therefore, she plotted with Jacob to deceive Isaac and have him pass the blessing on to Jacob. Remember: Isaac was blind and unable to see; therefore Jacob was able to deceive Isaac and receive the blessing.

> **"And Jacob went near unto Isaac his father; and he felt him, and said, The voice is Jacob's voice, but the hands are the hands of Esau. And he discerned him not, because his hands were hairy, as his brother Esau's hands: so he blessed him. And he said, Art thou my very son Esau? And he said, I am. And he said, Bring it near to me, and I will eat of my son's venison, that my soul may bless thee. And he brought it near to him, and he did eat: and he brought him wine, and he drank. And his father Isaac said unto him, Come near now, and kiss me, my son. And he came near, and kissed him: and he smelled the smell of his raiment, and blessed him, and said See, the smell of my son is as the smell of a field which the LORD hath blessed: Therefore God give thee of the dew of heaven, and the fatness of the earth, and plenty of corn and wine: let people serve thee, and nations bow down to thee: be lord over thy brethren, and let thy mother's sons bow down to thee: cursed be every one that curseth thee, and blessed be he that blesseth thee" (Ge.27:22-29).**

⇒   Isaac refused to reverse the blessing when the deception was discovered. In the final analysis, he repented. He turned away from his own desires and did God's will.

"And Isaac trembled very exceedingly, and said, Who? where is he that hath taken venison, and brought it me, and I have eaten of all before thou camest, and have blessed him? yea, and he shall be blessed" (Ge.27:33).

2   (11:20) **Isaac—Faith:** (Isaac's faith was firm about the future despite sin.) At first, Isaac was unwilling to follow God and do as God had said. And his son Jacob set out to secure God's blessing by deception. Jacob was unwilling to wait upon God; he felt that he had to help God out even if it meant lying and deceiving. But in the end, Isaac repented: he believed God and he did God's will. He could have easily reversed his blessing, but he refused. He had reached the point where he knew that God's will had to be done. Therefore, he repented and turned from his own will to the will of God.

Note through all of this the strong faith in *things to come*. Isaac believed in the promises of God; he believed in the *promised seed* and the *promised land*. He never saw the promises fulfilled, not during his life upon this earth. He was only a pilgrim and sojourner on earth, never seeing the *promised land*. But he believed and held firm to his belief—so firm that he passed the blessing of God's promises down through his son Jacob. Isaac died, but he died as a man of faith, (as a man who repented and did God's will.)

"Blessed are they that mourn: for they shall be comforted" (Mt.5:4).

"I tell you, Nay: but, except ye repent, ye shall all likewise perish" (Lu.13:3).

"Repent ye therefore, and be converted, that your sins may be blotted out, when the times of refreshing shall come from the presence of the Lord" (Ac.3:19).

"Repent therefore of this thy wickedness, and pray God, if perhaps the thought of thine heart may be forgiven thee" (Ac.8:22).

"And the times of this ignorance God winked at; but now commandeth all men every where to repent" (Ac.17:30).

"If my people, which are called by my name, shall humble themselves, and pray, and seek my face, and turn from their wicked ways; then will I hear from heaven, and will forgive their sin, and will heal their land" (2 Chr.7:14).

"Let the wicked forsake his way, and the unrighteous man his thoughts: and let him return unto the LORD, and he will have mercy upon him; and to our God, for he will abundantly pardon" (Is.55:7).

"But if the wicked will turn from all his sins that he hath committed, and keep all my statutes, and do that which is lawful and right, he shall surely live, he shall not die" (Eze.18:21).

	K. Jacob's Faith: A Worshipping Faith, 11:21
1. A faith that believed God's promises 2. A faith that worshipped God in the face of death	21 By faith Jacob, when he was a dying, blessed both the sons of Joseph; and worshipped, *leaning* upon the top of his staff.

DIVISION IV

THE SUPREME AUTHOR OF FAITH: JESUS CHRIST, GOD'S SON, 10:19–11:40

K.   Jacob's Faith: A Worshipping Faith, 11:21

(11:21) **Introduction**: Jacob never saw the promised land given to Israel. In fact, he saw the reverse. His family was forced to Egypt because of famine. Yet he continued to worship God, ever believing and passing on God's promise—even as he was dying.

1. A faith that believed God's promises (v.21).
2. A faith that worshipped God in the face of death (v.21).

1 (11:21) **Jacob—Faith**: Jacob's faith was a faith that believed God's promises and worshipped despite death. The story in the Old Testament is as follows:

> "And it came to pass after these things, that one told Joseph, Behold, thy father is sick: and he took with him his two sons, Manasseh and Ephraim. And one told Jacob, and said, Behold, thy son Joseph cometh unto thee: and Israel strengthened himself, and sat upon the bed. And Jacob said unto Joseph, God Almighty appeared unto me at Luz in the land of Canaan, and blessed me, And said unto me, Behold, I will make thee fruitful, and multiply thee, and I will make of thee a multitude of people; and will give this land to thy seed after thee for an everlasting possession. And now thy two sons, Ephraim and Manasseh, which were born unto thee in the land of Egypt before I came unto thee into Egypt, are mine; as Reuben and Simeon, they shall be mine. And thy issue, which thou begettest after them, shall be thine, and shall be called after the name of their brethren in their inheritance....And Joseph took them both, Ephraim in his right hand toward Israel's left hand, and Manasseh in his left hand toward Israel's right hand, and brought them near unto him. And Israel stretched out his right hand, and laid it upon Ephraim's head, who was the younger, and his left hand upon Manasseh's head, guiding his hands wittingly; for Manasseh was the firstborn. And he blessed Joseph, and said, God, before whom my fathers Abraham and Isaac did walk, the God who fed me all my life long unto this day, the angel which redeemed me from all evil, bless the lads; and let my name be named on them, and the name of my fathers Abraham and Isaac; and let them grow into a multitude in the midst of the earth" (Ge.48:1-6, 13-16).

Note two significant facts.

1. Jacob was dying when this event took place. He had lived a long life upon earth.
2. Jacob blessed both of the sons of Joseph; that is, he passed on the promises of God to them. He gave them an inheritance in the *land of promise* and in the *promised seed*. They had been born in Egypt; nevertheless, he passed the blessing of the promise down through them.

2 (11:21) **Jacob—Faith—Worship**: Jacob worshipped even while he was dying, worshipped leaning upon his staff. The idea is that he was weak and frail, almost bedridden, finding it difficult to walk and move about. But he continued to arise and worship God, believing in the *promised land* and *promised seed* up until the very end.

The point is striking. Here was a man who never saw the promised land given to him. In fact, he saw the reverse. He and his family were forced out of Canaan (Palestine) and into Egypt because of famine. Yet, he continued to worship God, ever believing and passing on God's promises—even up to the very end, the end of death itself.

> "Wherefore, sirs, be of good cheer: for I believe God, that it shall be even as it was told me" (Ac.27:25).
> "But without faith it is impossible to please him: for he that cometh to God must believe that he is, and that he is a rewarder of them that diligently seek him" (He.11:6).
> "Even so faith, if it hath not works, is dead, being alone" (Js.2:17).

"The LORD redeemeth the soul of his servants: and none of them that trust in him shall be desolate" (Ps.34:22).

"Trust in the LORD, and do good; so shalt thou dwell in the land, and verily thou shalt be fed" (Ps.37:3).

"Commit thy way unto the LORD; trust also in him; and he shall bring it to pass" (Ps.37:5).

"Trust in the LORD with all thine heart; and lean not unto thine own understanding" (Pr.3:5).

"Thou wilt keep him in perfect peace, whose mind is stayed on thee: because he trusteth in thee. Trust ye in the LORD for ever: for in the LORD JEHOVAH is everlasting strength" (Is.26:3-4).

	L. Joseph's Faith: An Undying Faith, 11:22
1. A faith that believed despite hard circumstances, see Ge. 37–40	22 By faith Joseph, when he died, made mention of the departing of the children of Israel; and gave commandment concerning his bones.
2. A faith that acted despite the impossible	

DIVISION IV

THE SUPREME AUTHOR OF FAITH: JESUS CHRIST, GOD'S SON, 10:19–11:40

L.   Joseph's Faith: An Undying Faith, 11:22

(11:22) **Introduction**: Joseph was a prince among a world of men. His life of faith is a life that should be studied and followed by all. The faith of Joseph was an undying faith.

1. A faith that believed despite hard circumstances (v.22).
2. A faith that acted despite the impossible (v.22).

1 (11:22) **Joseph—Faith**: Joseph's faith was faith that believed despite adverse circumstances. If ever a person should have lost faith, it was Joseph.

⇒ As a young man, he had been sold as a slave into Egypt, and note: it was his own brothers who had sold him (Ge.37:23f).
⇒ While a slave, he was falsely accused by his master's wife of trying to seduce her. He had rejected her advances, choosing to follow God in living righteously rather than to enjoy the fruits of sin for a season (Ge.39:7).
⇒ He suffered imprisonment because the wife falsely charged him with assault. He suffered a long imprisonment for living righteously (Ge.39:14f).
⇒ He lived righteously and ministered to people in prison even when they ignored, neglected, and forgot him (Ge.40:14f).

The point to note is this: Joseph never lost his faith in the promises of God. He believed and followed God no matter the circumstances and no matter what it cost him. He was a man of God in a foreign land, a man who demonstrated an undying faith.

2 (11:22) **Joseph—Faith**: Joseph had a faith that acted despite the impossible. This was Joseph's great act of faith. After so many years in a foreign land, he still proclaimed the great promise of God: he believed beyond question that God was going to fulfill His promises:

⇒ He believed that God had chosen his family to be the *promised seed*.
⇒ He believed that God was going to give the *promised land* to his family.

Joseph was dying in a foreign land with his family finally settled and rooted in the land of Goshen, Egypt. Yet he believed the impossible: that God would be moving his family back to Palestine and eventually give them the promised land. Therefore, he commanded that his bones be taken back when the nation of his family returned to the land.

Joseph's faith was an undying faith. His body was dying, but not his faith in God and in God's promises. He knew that he would rest in the promised land of God.

"He that endureth to the end shall be saved" (Mt.10:22).
"For whether we live, we live unto the Lord; and whether we die, we die unto the Lord: whether we live therefore, or die, we are the Lord's" (Ro.14:8).
"For he that soweth to his flesh shall of the flesh reap corruption; but he that soweth to the Spirit shall of the Spirit reap life everlasting" (Ga.6:8).
"These all died in faith, not having received the promises, but having seen them afar off, and were persuaded of them, and embraced them, and confessed that they were strangers and pilgrims on the earth" (He.11:13).
"Wherefore lay apart all filthiness and superfluity of naughtiness, and receive with meekness the engrafted word, which is able to save your souls" (Js.1:21).
"The Lord is not slack concerning his promise, as some men count slackness; but is longsuffering to us-ward, not willing that any should perish, but that all should come to repentance" (2 Pe.3:9).
"And I heard a voice from heaven saying unto me, Write, Blessed are the dead which die in the Lord from henceforth: Yea, saith the Spirit, that they may rest from their labours; and their works do follow them" (Re.14:13).
"Yea, though I walk through the valley of the shadow of death, I will fear no evil: for thou art with me; thy rod and thy staff they comfort me" (Ps.23:4).
"Precious in the sight of the LORD is the death of his saints" (Ps.116:15).
"The wicked is driven away in his wickedness: but the righteous hath hope in his death" (Pr.14:32).

	M. Moses' Parents' Faith: A Loving, Fearless Faith, 11:23
1. A faith that obeyed their hearts	23 By faith Moses, when he was born, was hid three months of his parents, because they saw *he was* a proper child; and they were not afraid of the king's commandment.
2. A faith that was fearless despite opposition	

DIVISION IV

THE SUPREME AUTHOR OF FAITH: JESUS CHRIST, GOD'S SON, 10:19–11:40

M. Moses' Parents' Faith: A Loving, Fearless Faith, 11:23

(11:23) **Introduction**: the parents of Moses are an excellent example of an unknown married couple who had great faith in God. They were just common, ordinary folk within their community, yet they believed God and had a strong faith in Him. Their faith stands as a dynamic example of a loving, fearless faith.
    1. A faith that obeyed their hearts (v.23).
    2. A faith that was fearless despite opposition (v.23).

1 (11:23) **Faith—Moses, Parents of**: the parents of Moses had a faith that obeyed their hearts. What happened was this: generation after generation had passed since Joseph, Jacob, and his sons had gone down to Egypt to settle in the land of Goshen, Egypt. The people, the Israelites, had reproduced so much that they had become a large nation of people, so large that the new king of Egypt felt threatened by them. This was when Israel became slaves to the Egyptians. The king, who did not know Joseph, took the initial step of enslaving them, thinking that he could slow down their reproduction through slavery (Ex.1:8). However, the children of Israel continued to multiply rather rapidly, and the king felt more and more threatened. Finally he decided to wipe them out by having all newborn sons killed at birth. This cruel plot was made the law of the land (see Ex.1:21-22).
    This is the background of what led Moses' parents to do what they did. Unquestionably, they loved God and loved their newborn child whom they named Moses. Their action shows this.
    Kenneth Wuest points out that the word "proper" (asteion) means "comely to God." Wuest says, "he was comely with respect to God"[1]. That is, God had His hand upon Moses, and apparently his parents realized it.
    One thing is sure: the parents knew that if all the male children were killed, then the *promised seed* and *promised land* of God could never be fulfilled. It is this that lies behind their saving Moses. They loved their child, yes, but they also loved God. It was their love for both their son and God that made them do what they did. Their love stirred them to believe that God would preserve their son and use him to fulfill God's promise of an eternal seed and eternal land for His people.

> "Jesus said unto him, Thou shalt love the Lord thy God with all thy heart, and with all thy soul, and with all thy mind" (Mt.22:37).
> "And we have known and believed the love that God hath to us. God is love; and he that dwelleth in love dwelleth in God, and God in him" (1 Jn.4:16).
> "Keep yourselves in the love of God, looking for the mercy of our Lord Jesus Christ unto eternal life" (Jude 21).
> "And thou shalt love the LORD thy God with all thine heart, and with all thy soul, and with all thy might" (De.6:5).
> "And now, Israel, what doth the LORD thy God require of thee, but to fear the LORD thy God, to walk in all his ways, and to love him, and to serve the LORD thy God with all thy heart and with all thy soul" (De.10:12).

2 (11:23) **Faith—Moses, Parents of**: the parents of Moses had a faith that was fearless despite opposition. As stated above, it was the law of the land that all newborn male children were to be killed at birth. Failure to obey the law most likely meant death to the law-breaker. The parents risked their lives in disobeying the law. But note what this verse says: "they were not afraid of the king's commandment." They trusted God to preserve the child, and they cast their own lives upon God's care. They knew they had to risk their lives in order to save their son and the promised seed and land of God.

---

1 Kenneth Wuest. *Hebrews*, Vol.2, p.205.

The point is this: the parents of Moses never received the promised land of God and they never saw the promised seed inherit the land. But they believed and trusted God, even in the face of a king's attempt to stamp out God's people and promise. They loved God and His promises and they believed God and His promises; therefore, they were willing to stake their lives upon Him and the *promised seed and land*.

"But without faith it is impossible to please him: for he that cometh to God must believe that he is, and that he is a rewarder of them that diligently seek him" (He.11:6).

"If any of you lack wisdom, let him ask of God, that giveth to all men liberally, and upbraideth not; and it shall be given him. But let him ask in faith, nothing wavering. For he that wavereth is like a wave of the sea driven with the wind and tossed" (Js.1:5-6).

"Even so faith, if it hath not works, is dead, being alone" (Js.2:17).

"For whatsoever is born of God overcometh the world: and this is the victory that overcometh the world, even our faith. Who is he that overcometh the world, but he that believeth that Jesus is the Son of God?" (1 Jn.5:4-5).

"The LORD redeemeth the soul of his servants: and none of them that trust in him shall be desolate" (Ps.34:22).

"Commit thy way unto the LORD; trust also in him; and he shall bring it to pass" (Ps.37:5).

"It is better to trust in the LORD than to put confidence in man" (Ps.118:8).

"Trust in the LORD with all thine heart; and lean not unto thine own understanding" (Pr.3:5).

"The rod and reproof give wisdom: but a child left to himself bringeth his mother to shame" (Pr.29:15).

"Trust ye in the LORD for ever: for in the LORD JEHOVAH is everlasting strength" (Is.26:4).

1. A sacrificial faith: He chose God & God's people rather than this world & its pleasures	N. Moses' Faith: A Self-Denying Faith, 11:24-28	the treasures in Egypt: for he had respect unto the recompence of the reward.	3. An enduring faith: He courageously looked to God instead of looking to men
	24 By faith Moses, when he was come to years, refused to be called the son of Pharaoh's daughter;	27 By faith he forsook Egypt, not fearing the wrath of the king: for he endured, as seeing him who is invisible.	
	25 Choosing rather to suffer affliction with the people of God, than to enjoy the pleasures of sin for a season;	28 Through faith he kept the passover, and the sprinkling of blood, lest he that destroyed the firstborn should touch them.	4. A saving faith: He believed God's message of salvation—symbolized in the Passover
2. An expectant faith: He looked to the reward, vv. 26, 27, 28	26 Esteeming the reproach of Christ greater riches than		

DIVISION IV

THE SUPREME AUTHOR OF FAITH: JESUS CHRIST, GOD'S SON, 10:19–11:40

N. Moses' Faith: A Self-Denying Faith, 11:24-28

(11:24-28) **Introduction**: following Christ is not easy, not if a person is going to truly follow Him. Why? Because His call is contrary to what most people think. His call is a call to love, joy, and peace, yes; but it is not a call to a life of ease, comfort, and plenty. The call of Christ is not to physical and material health and wealth. Contrariwise, the call of Christ is to a life of self-denial and sacrifice. If a person is going to follow Christ, it costs him everything he is and has. And Christ makes no exceptions (see outline and notes—Mt.19:16-22; 19:23-26; 19:27-30). Moses is a prime example of a man who gave up all that the world had to offer in order to follow God and His promises. His faith was a self-denying faith.

1. A sacrificial faith: he chose God and God's people rather than this world and its pleasures (vv.24-25).
2. An expectant faith: he looked to the reward (vv.26-28).
3. An enduring faith: he courageously looked to God instead of looking to men (v.27).
4. A saving faith: he believed God's message of salvation—symbolized in the Passover (v.28).

[1] (11:24-25) **Moses—Faith**: first, the faith of Moses was a sacrificial faith, a faith that chose God and God's people rather than this world and its pleasures. Remember: when Moses was born, the king of Egypt had issued a law that all newborn male children of Israel were to be killed. He had done this because he feared Israel was growing so rapidly as a people that they were becoming a threat to the security of Egypt. The parents of Moses, acting in faith, had hid Moses down by the river in a small boat-like basket. Moses was only three months old. His parents knew that Pharaoh's daughter bathed there, and they *sensed in hope* that she would find the child, feel compassion, and keep and rear him. This she did. Moses was reared as a prince in Pharaoh's court. Jewish tradition even says that his daughter was the only child Pharaoh had and that she herself was childless. If this is accurate, it means that Moses was, as tradition says, the heir to the throne of Egypt[1]. In either case, Moses was a prince, the son of the daughter of Pharaoh. He had everything that a person on earth could ever want:

⇒ education and knowledge
⇒ fame and wealth
⇒ possessions and estates
⇒ power and authority
⇒ position and duty
⇒ purpose and responsibility
⇒ a home and love (Pharaoh's daughter must have loved Moses to stand against Egyptian law to save him as a child.)

But Moses gave it all up. He sacrificed everything for God and His promises, the *promised seed* and *promised land*. The day came when Moses had to make the most critical decision of his life. He faced as large a crisis as any man could face. Was he going to be identified as an Egyptian all the days of his life or was he going to become identified with the people of God? Was he going to pursue the pleasures of Egypt and this world or pursue God and His promises? When Moses was forty years old, he faced the crisis and made the decision (Ac.7:23). In the words of Scripture:

> **"And it came to pass in those days, when Moses was grown, that he went out unto his brethren, and looked on their burdens: and he spied an Egyptian smiting a Hebrew, one of his brethren. And he looked this way and that way, and when he saw that there was no man, he slew the Egyptian, and hid him in the sand" (Ex.2:11-12).**

---

1 Thomas Hewitt. *The Epistle to the Hebrews*. "Tyndale New Testament Commentaries." (Grand Rapids, MI: Eerdmans Publishing Co., 1970), p.180. *Matthew Henry's Commentary*, Vol.6, p.947.

This was a scene that Moses had often seen during his forty years as an Egyptian prince. But apparently this was the final straw; he had seen enough of the mistreatment of his people. He made the decision that launched a number of decisions—decisions that were to show that he was rejecting Egypt and the world and identifying himself with God's people.

The point is this: Moses gave up all the pleasures and enjoyment of Egypt and the world—gave it all up. He sacrificed everything for God and His people, the very people who had been given the hope for *the promised seed and the promised land*.

As these two verses of Hebrews say:

> **"[Aroused] by faith Moses, when he had grown to maturity and become great, refused to be called the son of Pharaoh's daughter, because he preferred rather to share the oppression (suffer the hardships) and bear the shame of the people of God than to have the fleeting enjoyment of a sinful life" (vv.24-25, Amplified New Testament).**

Thought 1. Moses knew what he was doing. The decision to do what he could to stop the abuse of God's people was not the rash decision of youth. Moses was forty years old, engaged in the midst of the daily duties and power of ruling. He made his decision and acted, but as the next verse shows, only after much thought.

Thought 2. The Expositor's Greek Testament has an excellent statement on this point: "the significance and source of this refusal lay in his preferring to suffer ill-usage with God's people rather than to have a short-lived enjoyment of sin....it was because they were God's people, not solely because they were of his blood, that Moses threw in his lot with them. It was this that illustrated his faith. He believed that God would fulfill His promise to His people, little likelihood as at present there seemed to be of any great future for his race. On the other hand there was...the enjoyment which was within his reach if only he committed the sin of denying his people and renouncing their future as promised by God."[2]

> **"Then said Jesus unto his disciples, If any man will come after me, let him deny himself, and take up his cross, and follow me. For whosoever will save his life shall lose it: and whosoever will lose his life for my sake shall find it" (Mt.16:24-25).**
> **"Jesus said unto him, If thou wilt be perfect, go and sell that thou hast, and give to the poor, and thou shalt have treasure in heaven: and come and follow me" (Mt.19:21).**
> **"So likewise, whosoever he be of you that forsaketh not all that he hath, he cannot be my disciple" (Lu.14:33).**
> **"Let no man seek his own, but every man another's wealth" (1 Co.10:24).**
> **"For if ye live after the flesh, ye shall die: but if ye through the Spirit do mortify the deeds of the body, ye shall live" (Ro.8:13).**
> **"We then that are strong ought to bear the infirmities of the weak, and not to please ourselves" (Ro.15:1).**

2 (11:26) **Moses—Faith**: second, the faith of Moses was an expectant faith, a faith that looked to the reward. Moses believed in the promises which God had given to Abraham and his people, the promised seed and the promised land. (See notes—He.11:8-10; 11:13-16 for more discussion.) The word "esteeming" means that he considered and thought about the matter; he made a deliberate decision to suffer with his people and to inherit the promises God had made to them rather than to enjoy the riches of Egypt. This means...

*   that he chose the sufferings of Christ, the promised seed of the Savior, over the riches of Egypt
*   that he considered the reward of God's promise to Israel greater than the reward of earthly riches

William Barclay explains what Moses did in practical terms:

> *Moses was the man who gave up all earthly glory for the sake of the people of God. Christ gave up His glory for men. He became despised and rejected; He abandoned the glory of heaven for the buffets and the scourging and the shame inflicted by men. Moses in his day and generation shared in the sufferings of Christ. Moses was the man who chose the loyalty that led to suffering rather than the ease which led to earthly glory. He would rather suffer for the right than enjoy luxury with the wrong. He knew that the prizes of earth were contemptible compared with the ultimate reward of God.*[3]

Without question, Moses believed in the promises of God to Israel:

⇒ that Israel was the promised seed, the very people through whom God would send the Messiah, the Savior of the world.

⇒ that Israel would inherit the promised land of eternal rest with God. Moses turned away from the riches of the world for the rewards of God's promises.

2 Marcus Dods. *The Epistle to the Hebrews*. "The Expositor's Greek Testament," Vol.14. (Grand Rapids, MI: Eerdmans Publishing Co., 1970), p.360.
3 William Barclay. *The Letter to the Hebrews*, p.178.

"He considered the contempt and abuse and shame [borne for] the Christ, the Messiah [Who was to come], to be greater wealth than all the treasures of Egypt, for he looked forward and away to the reward (recompense)" (v.26, Amplified New Testament).

"Blessed are ye, when men shall revile you, and persecute you, and shall say all manner of evil against you falsely, for my sake" (Mt.5:11).

"And whosoever shall give to drink unto one of these little ones a cup of cold water only in the name of a disciple, verily I say unto you, he shall in no wise lose his reward" (Mt.10:42).

"If we suffer, we shall also reign with him: if we deny him, he also will deny us" (2 Ti.2:12).

"For ye had compassion of me in my bonds, and took joyfully the spoiling of your goods, knowing in yourselves that ye have in heaven a better and an enduring substance" (He.10:34).

"And others had trial of cruel mockings and scourgings, yea, moreover of bonds and imprisonment" (He.11:36).

3 (11:27) **Moses—Faith**: third, the faith of Moses was an enduring faith, a faith that courageously looked to God rather than to men. This event is recorded in Exodus.

"And when he went out the second day, behold, two men of the Hebrews strove together: and he said to him that did the wrong, Wherefore smitest thou thy fellow? And he said, Who made thee a prince and a judge over us? intendest thou to kill me, as thou killedst the Egyptian? And Moses feared, and said, Surely this thing is known" (Ex.2:13-15).

Note: it seems that Moses fled because he feared Pharaoh; however, Hebrews says that he "forsook Egypt; not fearing the wrath of the king." Is this a contradiction? No, the answer is given in Acts:

"And when he was full forty years old, it came into his heart to visit his brethren the children of Israel. And seeing one of them suffer wrong, he defended him, and avenged him that was oppressed, and smote the Egyptian: for he supposed his brethren would have understood how that God by his hand would deliver them: but they understood not" (Ac.7:23-25).

This shows that Moses had apparently thought and known for years that he was to be the deliverer of Israel. It is highly probable that his own mother had taught him this when Pharaoh's daughter unknowingly made her the nurse to Moses (Ex.2:6-8). She certainly taught him the great promises of God to Abraham and Israel. Whatever the source, God's Spirit apparently moved upon Moses at an early age and stirred the sense and thoughts that he was to be the deliverer of his people; he was to lead them back to Israel. However, Moses went about it the wrong way. Nevertheless, he knew that God's will and purpose was for him to deliver his people. Note: Acts 7:25 says that Moses was planning to lead Israel in a rebellion against Egypt to free God's people. He did not fear Pharaoh; Moses was loaded with courage. However, when the people refused to follow him, he was left alone. He had to fear—fear in the sense of wisdom and discretion, not despondency and hopelessness. He had to fear in order to save his life.

The point is this: Moses sensed and knew his mission upon earth—that he was to free Israel in God's time. The people would not follow him then, but he believed that God would arouse the people to follow him in due time. As we find out, he kept on believing and endured in his belief for another forty years (Ac.7:30).

Thought 1. Imagine the terrible disappointment Moses must have felt. His people were suffering as slave-laborers under Egyptian bondage, and he had stepped forward to lead them in a rebellion for freedom. But they had rejected his leadership, and he had been forced to flee for his life. The disappointment must have been very heavy. But imagine this: Moses sensed and knew that God had called him to deliver His people Israel. He knew his calling. But there he was sitting in Midian, and he had sat there for *forty years* and God had not called him to go forth. How easily Moses could have lost faith in God. How easily he could have lost his sense of call. But he did not: he continued to believe in God and His promises. Moses endured in faith despite all the circumstances. What a dynamic example!

"Therefore, my beloved brethren, be ye stedfast, unmoveable, always abounding in the work of the Lord, forasmuch as ye know that your labour is not in vain in the Lord" (1 Co.15:58).

"And let us not be weary in well doing: for in due season we shall reap, if we faint not" (Ga.6:9).

"Seeing then that we have a great high priest, that is passed into the heavens, Jesus the Son of God, let us hold fast our profession. For we have not an high priest which cannot be touched with the feeling of our infirmities; but was in all points tempted like as we are, yet without sin. Let us therefore come boldly unto the throne of grace, that we may obtain mercy, and find grace to help in time of need" (He.4:14-16).

"Let us hold fast the profession of our faith without wavering; (for he is faithful that promised)" (He.10:23).

"Wherefore gird up the loins of your mind, be sober, and hope to the end for the grace that is to be brought unto you at the revelation of Jesus Christ" (1 Pe.1:13).

"Behold, I come quickly; hold that fast which thou hast, that no man take thy crown" (Re.3:11).

4 (11:28) **Moses—Faith**: fourth, the faith of Moses was a saving faith, a faith that believed God's message of salvation. This verse refers to the great day of deliverance and salvation for Israel. God had led Moses to prepare Israel and Egypt for the deliverance of His people. God was now ready to save His people from the bondage of Egypt (a symbol of the world). God had pronounced judgment (the taking of the firstborn) upon the people of Egypt for their injustices. As He prepared to execute the final judgment, those who believed God were instructed to slay a pure lamb and sprinkle its blood over the door posts of their homes. The blood of the innocent lamb would then serve as a sign that the coming judgment had already been carried out. When seeing the blood, God would *pass over* that house.

Symbolically, the Passover pictured the coming of Jesus Christ as the Savior. The lamb without blemish pictured His sinless life, and the blood sprinkled on the door posts pictured His blood shed for the believer (Ex.12:5; see Jn.1:29).

Note that God's method of salvation was the blood of the lamb spread over the door posts (see Ge.12:12-48. See DEEPER STUDY # 1—Lu.22:7.) Moses' great faith is clearly seen. He not only made the proper arrangements for escaping God's judgment on that dreadful night, but he spelled out that the Passover was to be observed each year thereafter. He never doubted God's planned salvation for His people. He never doubted that God would fulfill His promises, that He would give to Israel the *promised seed* and the *promised land*.

> **"Much more then, being now justified by his blood, we shall be saved from wrath through him"** (Ro.5:9).
>
> **"For whosoever shall call upon the name of the Lord shall be saved"** (Ro.10:13).
>
> **"For by grace are ye saved through faith; and that not of yourselves: it is the gift of God"** (Ep.2:8).
>
> **"And almost all things are by the law purged with blood; and without shedding of blood is no remission"** (He.9:22).
>
> **"Forasmuch as ye know that ye were not redeemed with corruptible things, as silver and gold, from your vain conversation received by tradition from your fathers; but with the precious blood of Christ, as of a lamb without blemish and without spot"** (1 Pe.1:18-19).

	O. Israel's Faith (Part I): A Delivering Faith, 11:29
1. A faith that obeyed God against insurmountable forces 2. A faith that delivered God's people & brought protection	29 By faith they passed through the Red sea as by dry *land:* which the Egyptians assaying to do were drowned.

DIVISION IV

THE SUPREME AUTHOR OF FAITH: JESUS CHRIST, GOD'S SON, 10:19–11:40

O. Israel's Faith (Part I): A Delivering Faith, 11:29

(11:29) **Introduction**: this verse deals with Israel crossing the Red Sea, a phenomenal miracle controlled entirely by God. But it took great faith for Israel to cross the Sea with two towering walls of water on both sides. This is a living example of strong faith in God, a delivering faith, the kind of faith that assures God's delivering power acting in our behalf.

1. A faith that obeyed God against insurmountable forces (v.29).
2. A faith that delivered God's people and brought protection (v.29).

1 (11:29) **Israel—Faith**: Israel's faith was a faith that obeyed God against insurmountable forces. The forces confronting Israel were threefold:

⇒ the pursuing army of the Egyptians
⇒ the Red Sea in front and the mountain ranges on both sides
⇒ their own murmuring and unbelief

The people were ever so frightened. They were hemmed in with no way to escape, and an enraged king and people were in hot pursuit. There was no chance that the Egyptian army would have taken any live prisoners because Egypt had lost all their firstborn sons to the death-angel. Israel was doomed and the people knew it. The odds were insurmountable unless God stepped in and delivered them.

Moses, God's leader, was aroused to believe God. He stepped forward and shouted to the people:

> **"Fear ye not, stand still, and see the salvation of the LORD, which he will show to you today: for the Egyptians whom ye have seen today, ye shall see them again no more for ever. The LORD shall fight for you, and ye shall hold your peace" (Ex.14:13-14).**

The salvation of the Lord was being proclaimed, and that message stirred faith in the hearts of the people. In obedience to God's command, Moses lifted up his rod and moved it across the face of the waters. When he did, a strong east wind began to blow over the face of the water. It blew so forcefully that the waters divided. Imagine the scene: two towering walls of water with a stretch of dry land running down between them. But the people's salvation was on the other side. If they could reach there, they were safe. They had been grumbling, yes; but the message of God's servant, Moses, had stirred them to believe God. Now they were beholding the power of God to remove the insurmountable odds. He had actually rolled the sea back and made a road of *dry land* for them to march across to safety. They believed God, and they began to march forth—marching in the faith of God who had promised that He would lead them to the promised land.

Thought 1. What a clear picture of salvation for people today! No matter the odds, God will overcome the odds and save us if we will only believe and begin to march forth following Christ, even as God commands.

> **"Jesus answered and said unto them, Verily I say unto you, If ye have faith, and doubt not, ye shall not only do this which is done to the fig tree, but also if ye shall say unto this mountain, Be thou removed, and be thou cast into the sea; it shall be done" (Mt.21:21).**
> **"There hath no temptation taken you but such as is common to man: but God is faithful, who will not suffer you to be tempted above that ye are able; but will with the temptation also make a way to escape, that ye may be able to bear it" (1 Co.10:13).**
> **"Who delivered us from so great a death, and doth deliver: in whom we trust that he will yet deliver us" (2 Co.1:10).**
> **"And the Lord shall deliver me from every evil work, and will preserve me unto his heavenly kingdom: to whom be glory for ever and ever" (2 Ti.4:18).**
> **"Forasmuch then as the children are partakers of flesh and blood, he also himself likewise took part of the same; that through death he might destroy him that had the power of death, that is, the devil; and deliver them who through fear of death were all their lifetime subject to bondage" (He.2:14-15).**
> **"The Lord knoweth how to deliver the godly out of temptations, and to reserve the unjust unto the day of judgment to be punished" (2 Pe.2:9).**

"The Lord is my strength and my shield; my heart trusted in him, and I am helped: therefore my heart greatly rejoiceth; and with my song will I praise him" (Ps.28:7).

"But I am poor and needy; yet the Lord thinketh upon me: thou art my help and my deliverer; make no tarrying, O my God" (Ps.40:17).

2 (11:29) **Israel—Faith**: Israel's faith was a faith that delivered and brought protection. The people believed God; therefore, they were delivered despite the insurmountable odds against them. But not only this: they were protected through the whole experience. Their enemies pursued them. It was night when Israel crossed the sea and when the Egyptian army reached the shore (Ex.14:21). The Egyptians were spiritually blind to God's working and were hardened in their sin. After all, the children of Israel were not an army, but a defenseless body of people fleeing the might and power of the greatest army in the world. The Egyptians saw no reason to rush behind the people of Israel and slaughter them. Therefore, the army acted blindly, rashly, and unthoughtfully. They went right in after Israel. But God protected those who believed and trusted Him. The east wind died down and the two walls of water closed in and covered the pursuing enemy, drowning every one of them. God's people were protected—completely protected by the hand of God.

Thought 1. God performed the miracle of salvation and deliverance for the people, but it was because of their faith. God's messenger proclaimed the salvation of God and the people believed and God worked in their behalf. He saved and protected them from their enemy—an enemy that had appeared insurmountable. God always provides a way of deliverance for those who believe.

"Jesus answered and said unto them, Verily I say unto you, If ye have faith, and doubt not, ye shall not only do this which is done to the fig tree, but also if ye shall say unto this mountain, Be thou removed, and be thou cast into the sea; it shall be done" (Mt.21:21).

"For God so loved the world, that he gave his only begotten Son, that whosoever believeth in him should not perish, but have everlasting life" (Jn.3:16).

"And it shall come to pass, that whosoever shall call on the name of the Lord shall be saved" (Ac.2:21).

"For whosoever shall call upon the name of the Lord shall be saved" (Ro.10:13).

"For by grace are ye saved through faith; and that not of yourselves: it is the gift of God: not of works, lest any man should boast" (Ep.2:8-9).

"But the salvation of the righteous is of the Lord: he is their strength in the time of trouble" (Ps.37:39).

"Behold, God is my salvation; I will trust, and not be afraid: for the Lord JEHOVAH is my strength and my song; he also is become my salvation" (Is.12:2).

"And it shall be said in that day, Lo, this is our God; we have waited for him, and he will save us: this is the Lord; we have waited for him, we will be glad and rejoice in his salvation" (Is.25:9).

"The Lord thy God in the midst of thee is mighty; he will save, he will rejoice over thee with joy; he will rest in his love, he will joy over thee with singing" (Zep.3:17).

	P. Israel's Faith (Part II): A Conquering Faith, 11:30
1. A faith that believed the unusual: At Jericho 2. A faith that endured, persevered for seven long days	30 By faith the walls of Jericho fell down, after they were compassed about seven days.

DIVISION IV

THE SUPREME AUTHOR OF FAITH: JESUS CHRIST, GOD'S SON, 10:19–11:40

P.   Israel's Faith (Part II): A Conquering Faith, 11:30

(11:30) **Introduction**: the faith of Israel was a conquering faith. This was the kind of faith Israel needed in conquering Jericho—a faith that God could give victory over insurmountable forces (see Ex.14:1f). This is also the kind of faith that any person needs—a conquering faith. We need a faith that God will give us victory over the insurmountable forces of life no matter what the forces are, even the force of death.

1. A faith that believed the unusual: at Jericho (v.30).
2. A faith that endured, persevered for seven long days (v.30).

1 (11:30) **Israel—Faith**: Israel's faith was a conquering faith. This is the story of Joshua leading the people of Israel against Jericho (Jos.6:1-20). The fall of the walls of Jericho is a well-known story. Jericho was a fortress, completely surrounded by a wall and apparently manned by a strong people. How was Israel to take the city? Humanly speaking, the task was utterly impossible. Their only hope was God, and God was willing to give them victory over their enemies. It was just a matter of whether or not they would believe and trust God for victory. God issued His command:

⇒ The people were to march around the walls of Jericho once a day for six days.
⇒ Seven priests were to lead the march with the ark of the covenant following and then the people following it.
⇒ The march was to be in total silence for six days.
⇒ On the seventh day, the people were to march around the city seven times. After the seventh march, the priests were to blow seven trumpets and the people were to shout as loud as they could.

Thought 1. God's instructions—His Word, His commandments—are to be obeyed. No matter how difficult the task or the mission, a person is to believe the Word and the promises of God. It is only as a person obeys that he will have the promises fulfilled in his life.

"Jesus said unto him, If thou canst believe, all things *are* possible to him that believeth" (Mk.9:23).
"And the Lord said, If ye had faith as a grain of mustard seed, ye might say unto this sycamine tree, Be thou plucked up by the root, and be thou planted in the sea; and it should obey you" (Lu.17:6).
"Verily, verily, I say unto you, He that believeth on me, the works that I do shall he do also; and greater *works* than these shall he do; because I go unto my Father" (Jn.14:12).
"But whoso looketh into the perfect law of liberty, and continueth *therein,* he being not a forgetful hearer, but a doer of the work, this man shall be blessed in his deed" (Js.1:25).
"Blessed *are* they that do his commandments, that they may have right to the tree of life, and may enter in through the gates into the city" (Re.22:14).
"Now therefore, if ye will obey my voice indeed, and keep my covenant, then ye shall be a peculiar treasure unto me above all people: for all the earth *is* mine" (Ex.19:5).
"O that there were such an heart in them, that they would fear me, and keep all my commandments always, that it might be well with them, and with their children for ever!" (De.5:29).
"And if thou wilt walk in my ways, to keep my statutes and my commandments, as thy father David did walk, then I will lengthen thy days" (1 K.3:14).

2 (11:30) **Believer—Faith—Obedience—Word of God**: Israel's faith endured and persevered for seven long days. God said that if the people believed His instructions and His promise, the walls of Jericho would fall down. Of course most of the citizens of Jericho would be on top of the wall because of the change of events on the seventh day, expecting this to be the day that Israel was going to attack.

The point to see is the strong faith in God and in His instructions and promise. The people clearly trusted God to conquer their enemies for them. And He did. He conquered the enemies because the people believed His instructions and promise.

Thought 1. God will conquer the enemies of any person if the person will just believe the instructions and promise of God. The instruction may seem unreasonable and appear foolish to the world. What Israel did must have seemed very foolish to the citizens of Jericho. But if a person will go ahead and do what God says, God will conquer his enemies even as He did for Jericho.

"What shall we then say to these things? If God be for us, who can be against us? He that spared not his own Son, but delivered him up for us all, how shall he not with him also freely give us all things? Who shall lay any thing to the charge of God's elect? It is God that justifieth. Who is he that condemneth? It is Christ that died, yea rather, that is risen again, who is even at the right hand of God, who also maketh intercession for us. Who shall separate us from the love of Christ? shall tribulation, or distress, or persecution, or famine, or nakedness, or peril, or sword? As it is written, For thy sake we are killed all the day long; we are accounted as sheep for the slaughter. Nay, in all these things we are more than conquerors through him that loved us. For I am persuaded, that neither death, nor life, nor angels, nor principalities, nor powers, nor things present, nor things to come, nor height, nor depth, nor any other creature, shall be able to separate us from the love of God, which is in Christ Jesus our Lord" (Ro.8:31-39).

"Now thanks be unto God, which always causeth us to triumph in Christ, and maketh manifest the savour of his knowledge by us in every place" (2 Co.2:14).

"Forasmuch then as the children are partakers of flesh and blood, he also himself likewise took part of the same; that through death he might destroy him that had the power of death, that is, the devil; and deliver them who through fear of death were all their lifetime subject to bondage" (He.2:14-15).

"For whatsoever is born of God overcometh the world: and this is the victory that overcometh the world, even our faith. Who is he that overcometh the world, but he that believeth that Jesus is the Son of God?" (1 Jn.5:4-5).

"Through thee will we push down our enemies: through thy name will we tread them under that rise up against us" (Ps.44:5).

"And the God of peace shall bruise Satan under your feet shortly. The grace of our Lord Jesus Christ be with you" (Ro.16:20).

"There hath no temptation taken you but such as is common to man: but God is faithful, who will not suffer you to be tempted above that ye are able; but will with the temptation also make a way to escape, that ye may be able to bear it" (1 Co.10:13).

"Submit yourselves therefore to God. Resist the devil, and he will flee from you" (Js.4:7).

"To him that overcometh will I grant to sit with me in my throne, even as I also overcame, and am set down with my Father in his throne" (Re.3:21).

	Q. Rahab's Faith: A Saving Faith, 11:31
1. A faith that believed in the God of Israel 2. A faith that saved	31 By faith the harlot Rahab perished not with them that believed not, when she had received the spies with peace.

DIVISION IV

THE SUPREME AUTHOR OF FAITH: JESUS CHRIST, GOD'S SON, 10:19–11:40

Q. Rahab's Faith: A Saving Faith, 11:31

(11:31) **Introduction**: this is a beautiful picture of saving faith. It is the picture of one of Christ's ancestors, the picture of a harlot who turned from her sin to live for God. And because she did, she was saved and became one of the great women of history in the eyes of God and believers everywhere.

1. A faith that believed in the God of Israel (v.31).
2. A faith that saved (v.31).

1 (11:31) **Rahab—Faith**: the faith of Rahab was a faith that believed in the God of Israel (See Jos.2:1-21; 6:17, 22-23, 25; Mt.1:5; Js.2:25). She was a harlot and a Canaanite, a woman who was the furthest thing from being a follower of God, but she experienced a phenomenal conversion and she became a strong believer. What happened was this.

Joshua sent two spies into Jericho to spy out the city. They were almost caught, but they found refuge in the house of a prostitute named Rahab. The armed soldiers had heard that the spies were hiding out in her house and they confronted her, but she hid and protected them. Why? Why would she lie to her people and protect the two Israelite strangers? Scripture says because she believed in the God of Israel. How could she have possibly believed in the God of Israel when she was not an Israelite and had never been taught about the God of Israel and His promises? Scripture tells us. In conversation with the two spies she said:

> **"I know that the Lord hath given you the land, and that your terror is fallen upon us, and that all the inhabitants of the land faint because of you. For we have heard how the Lord dried up the water of the Red Sea for you, when ye came out of Egypt; and what ye did unto the two kings of the Amorites, that were on the other side Jordan, Sihon and Og, whom ye utterly destroyed. And as soon as we had heard these things, our hearts did melt, neither did there remain any more courage in any man, because of you:** *for the Lord your God, He is God in heaven above, and in earth beneath"* (Jos.2:9-11).

Rahab believed what she had heard about the God of Israel—that He was the true and living God. When it was humanly impossible for Israel to conquer Jericho—when Israel had no modern weapons to make war—when there was not a chance in this world that Israel could be victorious—Rahab believed in the God of Israel and she acted upon that faith. She believed that the God of Israel would save His people and give them the promised land. Therefore, she saved the lives of the two Israelite spies.

> **"Oh how great is thy goodness, which thou hast laid up for them that fear thee; which thou hast wrought for them that trust in thee before the sons of men!"** (Ps.31:19).
> **"Many sorrows shall be to the wicked: but he that trusteth in the Lord, mercy shall compass him about"** (Ps.32:10).
> **"The Lord redeemeth the soul of his servants: and none of them that trust in him shall be desolate"** (Ps.34:22).
> **"Commit thy way unto the Lord; trust also in him; and he shall bring it to pass"** (Ps.37:5).
> **"It is better to trust in the Lord than to put confidence in man"** (Ps.118:8).
> **"Trust in the Lord with all thine heart; and lean not unto thine own understanding"** (Pr.3:5).
> **"The fear of man bringeth a snare: but whoso putteth his trust in the Lord shall be safe"** (Pr.29:25).
> **"Who is among you that feareth the Lord, that obeyeth the voice of his servant, that walketh in darkness, and hath no light? let him trust in the name of the Lord, and stay upon his God"** (Is.50:10).

2 (11:31) **Rahab—Faith**: the faith of Rahab was a faith that saved her and her family. Rahab asked the two men to save her and her family when they attacked the city.

> **"Now therefore, I pray you, swear unto me by the LORD, since I have showed you kindness, that ye will also show kindness unto my father's house, and give me a true token: and that ye will save alive**

my father, and my mother, and my brethren, and my sisters, and all that they have, and deliver our lives from death. And the men answered her, Our life for yours, if ye utter not this our business. And it shall be, when the LORD hath given us the land, that we will deal kindly and truly with thee. Then she let them down by a cord through the window: for her house was upon the town wall, and she dwelt upon the wall. And she said unto them, Get you to the mountain, lest the pursuers meet you; and hide yourselves there three days, until the pursuers be returned: and afterward may ye go your way. And the men said unto her, We will be blameless of this thine oath which thou hast made us swear. Behold, when we come into the land, thou shalt bind this line of scarlet thread in the window which thou didst let us down by: and thou shalt bring thy father, and thy mother, and thy brethren, and all thy father's household, home unto thee. And it shall be, that whosoever shall go out of the doors of thy house, his blood shall be on our head, if any hand be upon him. And if thou utter this our business, then we will be quit [free] of thine oath which thou hast made us to swear. And she said, According unto your words, so be it. And she sent them away, and they departed: and she bound the scarlet line in the window" (Jos.2:12-21).

Note: it was seeing the scarlet (red) thread that was to save Rahab. Also note that Rahab demanded that the men "swear to her by the Lord." She strongly believed that Israel would conquer Jericho despite the impossible odds against them. She believed in the God of Israel: that God was going to give Israel the promised land. And most important of all, she believed that her life and salvation rested with the Israelites, that is, with the God of Israel. She believed that the God of Israel could and would save her. Oliver Greene has an excellent picture on the scarlet thread and salvation:

> This presents a beautiful picture of salvation. Two spies made the promise, Rahab believed it; and even though a great host of Israelites were to move in upon the city, she believed that the scarlet thread was her assurance of protection. All the money in Jericho could not have purchased that scarlet thread, because it was Rahab's guarantee of preservation while others were destroyed through unbelief: 'And Joshua saved Rahab the harlot alive, and her father's household, and all that she had; and she dwelleth in Israel even unto this day; because she hid the messengers, which Joshua sent to spy out Jericho" (Jos.6:25).
> This is most interesting. The Word of God does not name the Israelites who befriended this woman of Jericho, but some noble soul in the land of Israel took her in, loved her, and gave her a new home; and as she lived among the Israelites she grew in grace, in faith, and in strength.
> We can easily believe that Rahab was an attractive woman, one who had a winning personality and the ability to make friends easily; but now she had something more: she had the Lord God in her heart. She was a new creation, a completely new woman.
> A young man in Israel fell in love with her and married her. (I like to think that this young man was one of the spies, but that is just supposition on my part. The Bible does not tell us who he was.) The record does prove, however, that Rahab became the wife of an Israelite and God blessed them, gave them a son, and they called his name Boaz.
> We read of Boaz in Ruth 2:1 that he was a "mighty man of wealth," and Matthew 1:5 tells us, "Salmon begat Booz (Boaz) of Rachab; and Booz begat Obed of Ruth; and Obed begat Jesse." Jesse was the father of David, and it was through the lineage of David that the Saviour came!
> You see, when God saves a harlot, a murderer, a liar, a thief - or even a good moral person, that one becomes a new creation with a new heart and a new life. God saves - He does not repair: "Therefore if any man be in Christ, he is a new creature: old things are passed away; behold, all things are become new" (II Co.5:17).[1]

Thought 1. Just imagine! Rahab was one of the human ancestors of the Savior Himself, Christ Jesus our Lord. What a glorious picture of the saving grace of God. And His mercy and grace are eternal: they are able to save any of us today no matter how much of a harlot, derelict, thief, murderer, adulterer, liar, fame-seeker, drug addict, leader, boaster, socialite, or materialist we are. Whether we would be considered to be down and out or of the upper crust within society, God can save us. No matter what we are or what we have done, God can save us if we will only believe and trust in His Son, the Lord Jesus Christ.

"**That whosoever believeth in him should not perish, but have eternal life. For God so loved the world, that he gave his only begotten Son, that whosoever believeth in him should not perish, but have everlasting life**" (Jn.3:15-16).
"**He that believeth on the Son hath everlasting life: and he that believeth not the Son shall not see life; but the wrath of God abideth on him**" (Jn.3:36).
"**Verily, verily, I say unto you, He that heareth my word, and believeth on him that sent me, hath everlasting life, and shall not come into condemnation; but is passed from death unto life**" (Jn.5:24).
"**And this is the will of him that sent me, that every one which seeth the Son, and believeth on him, may have everlasting life: and I will raise him up at the last day**" (Jn.6:40).
"**Jesus said unto her, I am the resurrection, and the life: he that believeth in me, though he were dead, yet shall he live**" (Jn.11:25).
"**I am come a light into the world, that whosoever believeth on me should not abide in darkness**" (Jn.12:46).

---

[1] Oliver Greene. *The Epistle of Paul the Apostle to the Hebrews*, p.504f.

"But these are written, that ye might believe that Jesus is the Christ, the Son of God; and that believing ye might have life through his name" (Jn.20:31).

"That if thou shalt confess with thy mouth the Lord Jesus, and shalt believe in thine heart that God hath raised him from the dead, thou shalt be saved. For with the heart man believeth unto righteousness; and with the mouth confession is made unto salvation" (Ro.10:9-10).

"And that from a child thou hast known the holy scriptures, which are able to make thee wise unto salvation through faith which is in Christ Jesus" (2 Ti.3:15).

	R. The Great Believers' Faith (Part I): A Heroic Faith, 11:32-34
1. The heroic faith of out-standing leaders: A faith that accepted incredible responsibility & that called upon God for great courage	32 And what shall I more say? for the time would fail me to tell of Gedeon, and *of* Barak, and *of* Samson, and *of* Jephthae; *of* David also, and Samuel, and *of* the prophets:
2. The reward of heroic faith a. Conquered kingdoms b. Worked righteousness c. Obtained promises d. Shut the mouths of lions e. Quenched fire f. Escaped the sword g. Grew powerful in battle h. Routed armies	33 Who through faith subdued kingdoms, wrought righteousness, obtained promises, stopped the mouths of lions, 34 Quenched the violence of fire, escaped the edge of the sword, out of weakness were made strong, waxed valiant in fight, turned to flight the armies of the aliens.

DIVISION IV

THE SUPREME AUTHOR OF FAITH: JESUS CHRIST, GOD'S SON, 10:19–11:40

R.   The Great Believers' Faith (Part I): A Heroic Faith, 11:32-34

(11:32-34) **Introduction**: heroic faith—this is a powerful picture of just what heroic faith is. It is a panoramic scene that glances back over the history of Israel highlighting the lives of some great men of faith—men who dared to believe God against unbelievable odds. And in every case their faith triumphed and won the victory.

1. The heroic faith of outstanding leaders: a faith that accepted incredible responsibility and that called upon God for great courage (v.32).
2. The reward of heroic faith (vv.33-34).

1   (11:32) **Faith—Hall of Fame**: the heroic faith of outstanding leaders. Note that these three verses discuss the faith of some outstanding leaders. The faith of believers in general is discussed in the next few verses (v.35-40). These particular leaders were true heroes of the faith. They had a faith...

- that led them to feel undeserving and that demonstrated humility
- that accepted incredible responsibility
- that showed undying courage
- that trusted and depended entirely upon God
- that conquered against all odds—unbelievable odds

1. There was the faith of Gideon (Jud.6:11f). Gideon was already a grown man when God called him (Jud.8:20), and he had apparently gained a reputation as a soldier by fighting against the terrorists acts of the Midianites (Jud.6:12). The terrorists' attacks against Israel had gotten so fierce and frequent that the people had to be on constant guard. They even had to work inside protective walls in order to get their work done (Jud.6:11). Note these facts:

⇒   The angel of the Lord called Gideon to take the lead and to save Israel.
⇒   Gideon felt unqualified. He was gripped with a sense of humility and unworthiness. However, God gave Gideon assurance after assurance.
⇒   Gideon finally believed God and God gave Gideon the Spirit of the LORD.
⇒   Gideon tested God's call and promise by putting out the well known test of the fleece (Jud.6:36-40). God again assured Gideon that he was His chosen vessel to save Israel.
⇒   Gideon believed God, and with three hundred hand-picked men he defied incredible odds and routed and defeated the Midianite army (Jud.7:1f).

The point is this: Gideon was an outstanding leader because of his great faith. Even before he launched the great campaign against the Midianites, he cried out to his three hundred hand-picked men: "Arise, for the LORD hath delivered into your hand the host of Midian" (Jud.7:15).

2. There was the heroic faith of Barak (Jud.4-5). When the call of God came to Barak to save Israel, the Canaanites had been attacking and oppressing Israel for twenty years. The commander-in-chief of the Canaanite army was Sisero.

Note these facts:
- ⇒ The call of God to Barak came through the prophetess Deborah.
- ⇒ Barak was already a soldier, but he hesitated, feeling incapable. He insisted that the prophetess of God go to battle by his side. When she agreed, he surrendered to God's call.
- ⇒ Barak faced incredible odds. Sisero, the commander-in-chief of the Canaanites, had over 900 chariots of iron and a massive army.
- ⇒ Barak believed God. He attacked with only 10,000 men and won an incredible victory.

How did Barak do it? By faith. He had a heroic faith in God. He did not act without God. He believed God, and because he believed, God gave him the victory.

3. There was the heroic faith of Samson (Jud.13-16). The angel of the Lord appeared to the mother of Samson and told her that she was to bear a son who was to save Israel from the Philistines. Samson was to be reared under the Nazarite vows of extreme discipline, self-denial, and control of the flesh. The purpose of the Nazarite vows was symbolic, to teach the people that they were to live lives of self-denial and dedication before God. Note these facts about Samson.
- ⇒ Samson was appointed by God and he was a devout servant of God: "the Spirit of the LORD began to move him" (Jud.13:25; see Jud.14:19).
- ⇒ Samson was a man who had a serious flaw and weakness throughout all of his life, a weakness of fleshly passion. He never repented of his fleshly passion nor did he live by his Nazarite vows, not consistently.
- ⇒ Samson was a man of unusual faith and courage. He single-handedly fought the Philistines with unbelievable exploits of strength time and again. And he always won the victory.

The point to note about Samson's life is this: despite Samson's life-long weakness of passion, when the time came, he alone believed God; he alone was available for God to use. Samson was sometimes weak and passionate, but all others were even weaker and had less if any faith. Samson alone was available to believe and trust God. He was a man of heroic faith.

Thought 1. Matthew Henry makes a statement that we must always realize: "True faith is acknowledged and accepted, even when mingled with many failings."[1]

4. There was the heroic faith of Jephthah (Jud.11:1-12:7). Jephthah was called by God to save Israel from the Ammonites. Note these significant facts.
- ⇒ Jephthah was a man who had known rejection all of his life. He was the son of a harlot, but he was taken and reared by his father. However, he was apparently rejected, taunted, and abused by his family and neighbors all during his childhood. He was finally driven away from his home into the desert in exile (Jud.11:1-3). There in the desert he became the leader of a group of fighting adventurers who protected surrounding villages from Ammonite terrorists.
- ⇒ Jephthah believed and accepted the call to fight and save Israel when it came (Jud.11:4-11). He made a covenant with the elders of his people "before the Lord" (Jud.11:11).
- ⇒ Jephthah sought God's presence and strength for victory by making a vow to God (Jos.11:30-31).
- ⇒ Jephthah did what God wanted him to do and saved Israel (Jos.11:33).
- ⇒ Jephthah kept his vow to God and had his daughter live as a virgin and dedicate her life to serve God.

The point to see is that Jephthah was a man of unusual faith and trust in God despite being rejected by his family and townsfolk. He was also a man of great humility who humbled himself to help save and rule the people in their great crisis. Jephthah was a man of heroic faith.

5. There was the heroic faith of David (1 S.16:1f). As the writer to Hebrews says, "Time would fail me to tell...of David" (v.32). David was unquestionably one of the greatest men of heroic faith who has ever lived. Note these facts:
- ⇒ David was chosen to be the King of Israel by God Himself when he was only a young shepherd boy (1 S.16:1f).

"The Spirit of the Lord came upon David from that day forward" (1 S.16:13).

- ⇒ David was *a boy of heroic faith*. He believed God in facing impossible situations. For example, a lion and a bear attacked his sheep and a giant of a man named Goliath led the Philistine army against Israel, but God honored the young boy's faith and gave David the victory in both situations.
- ⇒ David was *a young man of heroic faith*. He was feared and hated by Saul the King because he had been appointed to be the future king of Israel while only a young boy. Saul pursued David for years trying to kill him. David proved to be a young man of extraordinary trust in God as he lived in the wilderness and faced trial after trial and enemy after enemy.

---

1 *Matthew Henry's Commentary*, Vol.6, p.951.

⇒ David was *a man of heroic faith* in defeating enemy after enemy. He stretched the borders of Israel out farther than anyone else had ever done and brought Israel to the height of its glory as a nation.

⇒ David ruled Israel for forty years and proved *faithful throughout his whole life* with exception of the one or two year lapse with Bathsheba (2 S.11:1f).

The whole life of David is a challenging example of heroic faith to believers of every generation. Just think of the Psalms, how meaningful they are to us all. David wrote approximately 73 of the Psalms. He was also one of the ancestors of Christ (Mt.1:1).

6. There was the heroic faith of Samuel (1-2 Samuel). Samuel was both a judge and prophet of Israel. God called Samuel when he was only a young child, and Samuel followed the Lord all through his life. During his lifetime he was the lone figure of great faith among a people who rebelled against God and refused to follow Him in righteousness and holiness. He was a man of heroic faith in the midst of a faithless and unbelieving generation.

7. There was the heroic faith of the prophets. They were all men who sensed their unworthiness before God but who answered God's call. They faced every imaginable trial that can be thrown against a man by a wicked and sinful people. But despite all, they stood for righteousness and proclaimed the message of God, a message of hope for those who would repent and a message of judgment for those who continued to live wicked and evil lives. They were men who stood almost alone in facing generation after generation of unbelief and rebellion against God. They were men of heroic faith.

2 (11:33-34) **Faith, Reward**: there was the reward of heroic faith.

1. Heroic faith subdued kingdoms. This is clearly seen in the heroic faith of the leaders above. The point is this: true faith in God will stir God to give the victory over all enemies, no matter how formidable. God will even work miraculously to deliver the person or people who truly believe Him.

> "Through thee will we push down our enemies: through thy name will we tread them under that rise up against us" (Ps.44:5).
> "Righteousness exalteth a nation: but sin is a reproach to any people" (Pr.14:34).
> "And we know that all things work together for good to them that love God, to them who are the called according to his purpose" (Ro.8:28).
> "Who shall separate us from the love of Christ? shall tribulation, or distress, or persecution, or famine, or nakedness, or peril, or sword?...Nay, in all these things we are more than conquerors through him that loved us" (Ro.8:35, 37).
> "There hath no temptation taken you but such as is common to man: but God is faithful, who will not suffer you to be tempted above that ye are able; but will with the temptation also make a way to escape, that ye may be able to bear it" (1 Co.10:13).
> "Now thanks be unto God, which always causeth us to triumph in Christ, and maketh manifest the savour of his knowledge by us in every place" (2 Co.2:14).
> "For whatsoever is born of God overcometh the world: and this is the victory that overcometh the world, even our faith. Who is he that overcometh the world, but he that believeth that Jesus is the Son of God?" (1 Jn.5:4-5).
> "He that hath an ear, let him hear what the Spirit saith unto the churches; To him that overcometh will I give to eat of the tree of life, which is in the midst of the paradise of God" (Re.2:7).
> "He that hath an ear, let him hear what the Spirit saith unto the churches; To him that overcometh will I give to eat of the hidden manna, and will give him a white stone, and in the stone a new name written, which no man knoweth saving he that receiveth it" (Re.2:17).
> "And he that overcometh, and keepeth my works unto the end, to him will I give power over the nations" (Re.2:26).
> "He that overcometh, the same shall be clothed in white raiment; and I will not blot out his name out of the book of life, but I will confess his name before my Father, and before his angels" (Re.3:5).
> "Him that overcometh will I make a pillar in the temple of my God, and he shall go no more out: and I will write upon him the name of my God, and the name of the city of my God, which is new Jerusalem, which cometh down out of heaven from my God: and I will write upon him my new name" (Re.3:12).
> "To him that overcometh will I grant to sit with me in my throne, even as I also overcame, and am set down with my Father in his throne" (Re.3:21).
> "He that overcometh shall inherit all things; and I will be his God, and he shall be my son" (Re.21:7).

2. Heroic faith wrought righteousness. This means two things.
⇒ When the leaders above believed God, righteousness was wrought in their lives. Faith always works righteousness in the life of the believer.
⇒ When the leaders above believed God, they set a dynamic example of righteousness and they taught and preached righteousness. As a result, some people turned to God and began to live righteously themselves. Faith—even if it is the faith of only one person—always stirs others to believe God and to live righteously themselves.

"By the blessing of the upright the city is exalted: but it is overthrown by the mouth of the wicked" (Pr.11:11).

"Righteousness exalteth a nation: but sin is a reproach to any people" (Pr.14:34).

"It is an abomination to kings to commit wickedness: for the throne is established by righteousness" (Pr.16:12).

"Take away the wicked from before the king, and his throne shall be established in righteousness" (Pr.25:5).

"In righteousness shalt thou be established: thou shalt be far from oppression; for thou shalt not fear: and from terror; for it shall not come near thee" (Is.54:14).

"Blessed are they which do hunger and thirst after righteousness: for they shall be filled" (Mt.5:6).

"For I say unto you, That except your righteousness shall exceed the righteousness of the scribes and Pharisees, ye shall in no case enter into the kingdom of heaven" (Mt.5:20).

"Awake to righteousness, and sin not; for some have not the knowledge of God: I speak this to your shame" (1 Co.15:34).

"Stand therefore, having your loins girt about with truth, and having on the breastplate of righteousness" (Ep.6:14).

"Being filled with the fruits of righteousness, which are by Jesus Christ, unto the glory and praise of God" (Ph.1:11).

3. Heroic faith obtained promises. God did just what He had promised to each of the leaders above. He always fulfills His promises to everyone who believes Him. And note: just as with each of the leaders above, He gives the assurance that He will fulfill His promises.

"He [Abraham] staggered not at the promise of God through unbelief; but was strong in faith, giving glory to God; and being fully persuaded that, what he had promised, he was able also to perform" (Ro.4:20-21).

"For all the promises of God in him are yea, and in him Amen, unto the glory of God by us" (2 Co.1:20).

"Having therefore these promises, dearly beloved, let us cleanse ourselves from all filthiness of the flesh and spirit, perfecting holiness in the fear of God" (2 Co.7:1).

"Whereby are given unto us exceeding great and precious promises: that by these ye might be partakers of the divine nature, having escaped the corruption that is in the world through lust" (2 Pe.1:4).

"And this is the promise that he hath promised us, even eternal life" (1 Jn.2:25).

"And this is the confidence that we have in him, that, if we ask any thing according to his will, he heareth us: and if we know that he hear us, whatsoever we ask, we know that we have the petitions that we desired of him" (1 Jn.5:14-15).

4. Heroic faith stopped the mouths of lions. This was true of Samson (Jud.14:5-6), David (1 S.17:34-35), and Daniel (Da.6:22). The meaning for believers is this: God has the power to control the animals and nature of this world if believers will trust God. And even more importantly, God will deliver believers from the mouth of the lion which is Satan.

"Casting all your care upon him; for he careth for you. Be sober, be vigilant; because your adversary the devil, as a roaring lion, walketh about, seeking whom he may devour: whom resist stedfast in the faith, knowing that the same afflictions are accomplished in your brethren that are in the world" (1 Pe.5:7-9).

"And the Lord shall deliver me from every evil work, and will preserve me unto his heavenly kingdom: to whom be glory for ever and ever" (2 Ti.4:18).

"And deliver them who through fear of death were all their lifetime subject to bondage" (He.2:15).

"The Lord knoweth how to deliver the godly out of temptations, and to reserve the unjust unto the day of judgment to be punished" (2 Pe.2:9).

"For we have not an high priest which cannot be touched with the feeling of our infirmities; but was in all points tempted like as we are, yet without sin. Let us therefore come boldly unto the throne of grace, that we may obtain mercy, and find grace to help in time of need" (He.4:15-16).

"Let us draw near with a true heart in full assurance of faith, having our hearts sprinkled from an evil conscience, and our bodies washed with pure water. Let us hold fast the profession of our faith without wavering; (for he is faithful that promised)" (He.10:22-23).

5. Heroic faith quenched the violence of fire. This probably refers to the three Hebrew young men—Shadrack, Meshack, and Abednego—who refused to worship the state religion of Nebuchadnezar. Therefore, they were to be executed by being burned alive. However God saved them by performing a most fantastic miracle: He preserved them and kept the flames of fire from burning them (Da.3:17-27).

God is God. He can preserve a person through both the fiery flame of temptation and trial and the fiery flame of persecution. In fact, God can preserve a person through anything. But note the prerequisite: faith in Him. We must believe God, really believe Him.

"And the Lord shall deliver me from every evil work, and will preserve me unto his heavenly kingdom: to whom be glory for ever and ever" (2 Ti.4:18).

"And the LORD commanded us to do all these statutes, to fear the LORD our God, for our good always, that he might preserve us alive, as it is at this day" (De.6:24).

"O love the LORD, all ye his saints: for the LORD preserveth the faithful, and plentifully rewardeth the proud doer" (Ps.31:23).

"For the LORD loveth judgment, and forsaketh not his saints; they are preserved for ever: but the seed of the wicked shall be cut off" (Ps.37:28).

"He keepeth the paths of judgment, and preserveth the way of his saints" (Pr.2:8).

"Fear thou not; For I am with thee: be not dismayed; for I am thy God: I will strengthen thee; yea, I will help thee; yea, I will uphold thee with the right hand of my righteousness" (Is.41:10).

"And even to your old age I am he; and even to hoar [gray] hairs will I carry you: I have made, and I will bear; even I will carry, and will deliver you" (Is.46:4).

"Thus saith the LORD, In an acceptable time have I heard thee, and in a day of salvation have I helped thee: and I will preserve thee, and give thee for a covenant of the people, to establish the earth, to cause to inherit the desolate heritages" (Is.49:8).

6. Heroic faith escaped the edge of the sword. David escaped the sword of Goliath (1 S.17:49-51); Elisha escaped the sword of the king of Israel (1 K.6:30-31). Prophet after prophet was delivered from martyrdom time after time by the power of God.

God will deliver the believer from violence and death unless God wills to use the martyrdom of the dear child as a testimony and wills to take His dear child on home to be with Him. God is able to deliver the person who truly believes Him. But remember: without faith in God, no person is delivered by God. Faith is the power that takes hold of the hand of God and brings about deliverance.

"But there shall not an hair of your head perish" (Lu.21:18).

"For the which cause I also suffer these things: nevertheless I am not ashamed: for I know whom I have believed, and am persuaded that he is able to keep that which I have committed unto him against that day" (2 Ti.1:12).

"Who are kept by the power of God through faith unto salvation ready to be revealed in the last time" (1 Pe.1:5).

"Now unto him that is able to keep you from falling, and to present you faultless before the presence of his glory with exceeding joy" (Jude 24).

"Because thou hast kept the word of my patience, I also will keep thee from the hour of temptation, which shall come upon all the world, to try them that dwell upon the earth" (Re.3:10).

"For the eyes of the LORD run to and fro throughout the whole earth, to show himself strong in the behalf of them whose heart is perfect toward him" (2 Chr.16:9).

"The angel of the LORD encampeth round about them that fear him, and delivereth them" (Ps.34:7).

"He shall cover thee with his feathers, and under his wings shalt thou trust: his truth shall be thy shield and buckler" (Ps.91:4).

"As the mountains are round about Jerusalem, so the LORD is round about his people from henceforth even for ever" (Ps.125:2).

7. Heroic faith brings strength out of weakness. Every one of the leaders above sensed unworthiness and weakness in serving God, but God strengthened them to conquer all the enemies and forces that stood against them.

"Then said I [Isaiah], Woe is me! for I am undone; because I am a man of unclean lips, and I dwell in the midst of a people of unclean lips: for mine eyes have seen the King, the LORD of hosts" (Is.6:5).

"Then said I [Jeremiah], Ah, Lord God! behold, I cannot speak: for I am a child" (Je.1:6).

"But God hath chosen the foolish things of the world to confound the wise; and God hath chosen the weak things of the world to confound the things which are mighty" (1 Co.1:27).

"And he said unto me, My grace is sufficient for thee: for my strength is made perfect in weakness. Most gladly therefore will I rather glory in my infirmities, that the power of Christ may rest upon me. Therefore I take pleasure in infirmities, in reproaches, in necessities, in persecutions, in distresses for Christ's sake: for when I am weak, then am I strong" (2 Co.12:9-10).

8. Heroic faith grows valiant in fight. True faith develops and stirs courage and strength. The person who truly believes in God knows that God is with him. He is actually stirred to fight and fight, even against unbelievable odds.

"God is my strength and power; and he maketh my way perfect....He teacheth my hands to war; so that a bow of steel is broken by mine arms" (2 S.22:33, 35).

"Be strong and of a good courage, fear not, nor be afraid of them: for the Lord thy God, he it is that doth go with thee; he will not fail thee, nor forsake thee" (De.31:6).

"Be strong and of a good courage: for unto this people shalt thou divide for an inheritance the land, which I sware unto their fathers to give them" (Jos.1:6).

"And Joshua said unto them, Fear not, nor be dismayed, be strong and of good courage: for thus shall the LORD do to all your enemies against whom ye fight" (Jos.10:25).

"Be ye therefore very courageous to keep and to do all that is written in the book of the law of Moses, that ye turn not aside therefrom to the right hand or to the left: that ye come not among these nations, these that remain among you; neither make mention of the names of their gods, nor cause to swear by them, neither serve them, nor bow yourselves unto them: but cleave unto the LORD your God, as ye have done unto this day. For the LORD hath driven out from before you great nations and strong: but as for you, no man hath been able to stand before you unto this day. One man of you shall chase a thousand: for the LORD your God, he it is that fighteth for you, as he hath promised you" (Jos.23:6-10).

"Be of good courage, and let us behave ourselves valiantly for our people, and for the cities of our God: and let the LORD do that which is good in his sight" (1 Chr.19:13).

"Then shalt thou prosper, if thou takest heed to fulfill the statutes and judgments which the LORD charged Moses with concerning Israel: be strong, and of good courage; dread not, nor be dismayed" (1 Chr.22:13).

"And David said to Solomon his son, Be strong and of good courage, and do it: fear not, nor be dismayed: for the LORD God, even my God, will be with thee; he will not fail thee, nor forsake thee, until thou hast finished all the work for the service of the house of the LORD" (1 Chr.28:20).

"I will not be afraid of ten thousands of people, that have set themselves against me round about" (Ps.3:6).

"Though a host should encamp against me, my heart shall not fear: though war should rise against me, in this will I be confident" (Ps.27:3).

"Thou shalt not be afraid for the terror by night; nor for the arrow that flieth by day" (Ps.91:5).

"The Lord is on my side; I will not fear: what can man do unto me?" (Ps.118:6).

"When thou liest down, thou shalt not be afraid, yea, thou shalt lie down, and thy sleep shall be sweet" (Pr.3:24).

"Behold, God is my salvation; I will trust, and not be afraid: for the Lord JEHOVAH is my strength and my song; he also is become my salvation" (Is.12:2).

1. There was the enduring faith of believers	**S. The Great Believers' Faith (Part II): An Enduring Faith, 11:35-40**	sword: they wandered about in sheepskins and goatskins; being destitute, afflicted, tormented;	e. Some were treated in the most inhumane way imaginable
a. Some women received their dead raised	35 Women received their dead raised to life again: and others were tortured, not accepting deliverance; that they might obtain a better resurrection:	38 (Of whom the world was not worthy:) they wandered in deserts, and *in* mountains, and *in* dens and caves of the earth.	
b. Some were tortured			
c. Some endured trials of mockery, scourging, chains, & imprisonment	36 And others had trial of *cruel* mockings and scourgings, yea, moreover of bonds and imprisonment:	39 And these all, having obtained a good report through faith, received not the promise:	2. There was the reward of enduring faith
d. Some were martyred	37 They were stoned, they were sawn asunder, were tempted, were slain with the	40 God having provided some better thing for us, that they without us should not be made perfect.	a. Receiving God's approval & a great historic witness
			b. Receiving the promised Seed or Messiah & the promised land, vv. 39-40

DIVISION IV

THE SUPREME AUTHOR OF FAITH: JESUS CHRIST, GOD'S SON, 10:19–11:40

S. The Great Believers' Faith (Part II): An Enduring Faith, 11:35-40

(11:35-40) **Introduction**: this is the powerful picture of what enduring faith is. It is a faith that endures even martyrdom if necessary. This passage is a panoramic scene that glances back over the history of the Old Testament and highlights the enduring faith of God's people.

1. There was the enduring faith of believers (vv.35-38).
2. There was the reward of enduring faith (vv.39-40).

[1] (11:35-38) **Faith—Endurance**: there was the enduring faith of believers. Note: no names are mentioned in these verses. As verse 35 indicates, they were the women and men of every day life who were not necessarily leaders, but who had one distinctive trait: they believed God and their faith in God was strong. They endured in faith no matter what attacked them. They never accepted defeat; therefore, they were never defeated. They never denied God; therefore, they were never denied by God. They never lost hope; therefore, they were never left hopeless. They endured in faith. No matter the circumstance, difficulty, threat, injury, pain, torture, or form of execution and death, they endured and held fast to their faith and profession in God.

1. Some believers—women—received their dead raised to life again. This is an astounding fact, that some believers could have faith strong enough to have their children raised from the dead. Yet it is true. The Old Testament gives two examples; perhaps there were others, but they are not recorded in the Scripture (1 K.17:17-24; 2 K.4:18-37). In the New Testament Christ raised several people from the dead (see Mt.9:18-34; Lu.7:11-17; Jn.11:41-46). The point is this: enduring faith—faith that will not let God go—will conquer anything including death. It is not the normal experience for God to raise people from the dead, but He has done it, and He did it because the mothers (and fathers) believed God. If they had not believed God, nothing would have ever happened. They would have just resigned themselves to the death. But they believed God and God raised them. Why? Why these few isolated instances? Why would God raise these and not raise others? Does this mean that some had weak faith and some had strong faith? No, not necessarily. The faith of some persons, of course, is stronger than the faith of others. But some have sought God with just as strong a faith as others, yet they received a different answer. Their dead children were not raised. Why?

⇒ Because circumstances were different. God could teach them more about Himself by strengthening them to go through the death and circumstances. In addition, their testimony to a lost and unbelieving world would sometimes be stronger by experiencing the sorrow and grief of death.

We must always remember that God knows best, even in the death of children. He knows how to make us stronger and how to bear a strong testimony to the world through all the circumstances of life, even through death. But note: God cannot strengthen us, raise the dead, nor do anything else apart from faith—faith that endures. We must believe in God and His power and love, and we must endure in that belief. It was enduring faith that caused these women to receive their dead raised to life. And it will be enduring faith that will cause us to receive the provision of our needs from God.

2. Some believers were tortured, refusing to deny God. The word "tortured" (etumpanisthesan) means to beat or club to death or else to be put on the rack in order to make a person deny Christ. These dear believers suffered martyrdom for the name of Christ. They *refused to accept deliverance*. All they had to do was renounce Christ, but they refused. And note why: "that they might obtain a better resurrection." They had their eyes on the *promised land* of heaven and glory, of living forever and ever with God and Christ. They knew something that was critical, something that is critical for every person to know:

⇒ If they had denied their faith, they would have saved their lives upon earth for a few days, perhaps even for several more years. But eventually they would have died anyway—accident, disease, old age, or something would have consumed their body and snatched or drained the life out of it.

But not faith in God. God gives life—life eternal—to the soul of man. And these dear believers were not about to turn back and reject eternal life just to walk in this evil and dying world for a few more days or at most a few years. They had their eyes on a better resurrection and world—on the resurrection and world that is eternal, never ending, and that is with God and Christ forever and ever.

3. Some believers endured trials of mockings, scourgings, and being chained and imprisoned.
   ⇒ They were mocked: ridiculed, insulted, treated with contempt, and cursed.
   ⇒ They were scourged: beaten with rods, whips, and cords of leather straps with bone and metal chips tied to the end—beaten until they died or were near death.
   ⇒ They were chained hand and foot, sometimes for years (even Paul the apostle suffered this as well as so many of the other trials mentioned throughout this section).
   ⇒ They were imprisoned in the most horrendous dungeons or prisons in the history of men.

They suffered for their faith, refusing to deny God and Christ and the glorious hope of the *promised land*—of living forever and ever with God.

4. Some believers were martyred for their faith.
   ⇒ Some were stoned to death. They were cast to the ground and surrounded by a mob of executioners. The executioners took hand size stones and hurled them at the victim causing whatever excruciating pain they could to the vital parts of the person's body and then eventually crushing the head. (see Zechariah, 2 Chr.24:20f.)
   ⇒ Some were sawn asunder. Oliver Greene says the method used was to put a person in a hollow log and then to saw through the log and the person.[1]

These are horrible pictures of death, but they are just some of the ways the world in its madness against believers have slaughtered them for their faith. Note: the believers were "lured with tempting offers [to renounce their faith]" but they refused (Amplified New Testament). They chose to receive the eternal life of God rather than a few days upon this evil and dying world.

5. Some believers were treated in the most inhuman ways imaginable.
   ⇒ They were stripped of all clothing and forced to wander about in sheepskins and goatskins.
   ⇒ They were stripped of all possessions—had everything taken away and confiscated—their homes, property, money, everything. They were left utterly destitute and they were afflicted and tormented as much as possible as object lessons in order to stop anyone else from believing in God and Christ.
   ⇒ They were forced to wander about and find shelter wherever they could: in deserts, in mountains, and in the dens and caves of the earth.

But note the glorious declaration of Scripture: the world was not worthy of these precious people—the dear, dear believers who honored and worshipped God. The idea is this: the unbelievers of the world stripped them and confiscated everything that was *worth anything* on this earth. But the world—the whole world with all its people and all their wealth—was *not worthy* of a single one of these dear believers.

"**Blessed are ye, when men shall revile you, and persecute you, and shall say all manner of evil against you falsely, for my sake**" (Mt.5:11).
"**And ye shall be hated of all men for my name's sake: but he that endureth to the end shall be saved**" (Mt.10:22).
"**And every one that hath forsaken houses, or brethren, or sisters, or father, or mother, or wife, or children, or lands, for my name's sake, shall receive an hundredfold, and shall inherit everlasting life**" (Mt.19:29).
"**For we which live are alway delivered unto death for Jesus' sake, that the life also of Jesus might be made manifest in our mortal flesh**" (2 Co.4:11).
"**For unto you it is given in the behalf of Christ, not only to believe on him, but also to suffer for his sake**" (Ph.1:29).
"**Take, my brethren, the prophets, who have spoken in the name of the Lord, for an example of suffering affliction, and of patience**" (Js.5:10).
"**If ye were of the world, the world would love his own: but because ye are not of the world, but I have chosen you out of the world, therefore the world hateth you**" (Jn.15:19).
"**If the world hate you, ye know that it hated me before it hated you....If I had not come and spoken unto them, they had not had sin: but now they have no cloke for their sin**" (Jn.15:18, 22).
"**Yea, and all that will live godly in Christ Jesus shall suffer persecution**" (2 Ti.3:12).
"**But all these things will they do unto you for my name's sake, because they know not him that sent me**" (Jn.15:21).

---

1 Oliver Greene. *The Epistle of Paul the Apostle to the Hebrews*, p.514.

"They shall put you out of the synagogues: yea, the time cometh, that whosoever killeth you will think that he doeth God service. And these things will they do unto you, because they have not known the Father, nor me" (Jn.16:2-3).

"Remember the word that I said unto you, The servant is not greater than his lord. If they have persecuted me, they will also persecute you; if they have kept my saying, they will keep yours also" (Jn.15:20).

"These things have I spoken unto you, that ye should not be offended. They shall put you out of the synagogues: yea, the time cometh, that whosoever killeth you will think that he doeth God service. And these things will they do unto you, because they have not known the Father, nor me. But these things have I told you, that when the time shall come, ye may remember that I told you of them. And these things I said not unto you at the beginning, because I was with you" (Jn.16:1-4).

"That no man should be moved by these afflictions: for yourselves know that we are appointed thereunto" (1 Th.3:3).

"Marvel not, my brethren, if the world hate you" (1 Jn.3:13).

"Beloved, think it not strange concerning the fiery trial which is to try you, as though some strange thing happened unto you: but rejoice, inasmuch as ye are partakers of Christ's sufferings; that, when his glory shall be revealed, ye may be glad also with exceeding joy. If ye be reproached for the name of Christ, happy are ye; for the spirit of glory and of God resteth upon you: on their part he is evil spoken of, but on your part he is glorified" (1 Pe.4:12-14).

2 (11:39-40) **Faith—Reward**: there was the reward of enduring faith. The reward was twofold.

1. All the believers of the Old Testament obtained a good report and testimony. Their faith touched both God and man. Their faith was the light of the world; their lives pointed men to God, and their testimonies still do. Note: their faith touched God so much that He has recorded it forever in this chapter of Hebrews. And although their names are not mentioned for the world to honor, what is important *is stressed*, that is, their faith. It is not their names that would stir people; it is their faith. It is the faith of their lives that touches the hearts and lives of people. Their faith touches people of every generation and stirs them to be men and women of stronger faith. What a legacy to leave behind, a legacy of faith that stirs and encourages people to arise and trust God and to live righteously and godly and to make this a much better world for God.

"First, I thank my God through Jesus Christ for you all, that your faith is spoken of throughout the whole world" (Ro.1:8).

"For your obedience is come abroad unto all men. I am glad therefore on your behalf: but yet I would have you wise unto that which is good, and simple concerning evil" (Ro.16:19).

"For by it [faith] the elders obtained a good report" (He.11:2).

2. They had the glorious hope of the *promised land and the promised seed*. They died without receiving the promised seed. They never saw Christ born, crucified, resurrected, and exalted to the right hand of God the Father. They never saw their salvation secured by Christ, who was the very Son of God. They never saw the promise of the Messiah fulfilled. They died believing the promise, but they never knew exactly how their salvation was to be arranged.

But this is not true with us: we know. Christ has come; He has died and been resurrected and exalted to make all believers perfect and presentable to God the Father. The Old Testament believers looked forward to the Messiah; we look back upon Him. We are far more privileged. It has already happened; it is a historic fact: Christ Jesus our Lord has now died and been resurrected to make us all acceptable to God. All believers—both Old and New Testament believers—are covered by the death and resurrection of Jesus Christ. Faith in Him causes God to count us righteous and free from the guilt and judgment of sin. And being free of sin makes us perfect in God's eyes. But we must always remember: our righteousness and our perfection is in *Christ and in Christ alone*.

"For God so loved the world, that he gave his only begotten Son, that whosoever believeth in him should not perish, but have everlasting life. For God sent not his Son into the world to condemn the world; but that the world through him might be saved" (Jn.3:16-17).

"Therefore being justified by faith, we have peace with God through our Lord Jesus Christ" (Ro.5:1).

"And if ye be Christ's, then are ye Abraham's seed, and heirs according to the promise" (Ga.3:29).

"For the promise, that he should be the heir of the world, was not to Abraham, or to his seed, through the law, but through the righteousness of faith. For if they which are of the law be heirs, faith is made void, and the promise made of none effect" (Ro.4:13-14).

"By faith Abraham, when he was called to go out into a place which he should after receive for an inheritance, obeyed; and he went out, not knowing whither he went. By faith he sojourned in the land of promise, as in a strange country, dwelling in tabernacles with Isaac and Jacob, the heirs with him of the same promise: for he looked for a city which hath foundations, whose builder and maker is God....These all died in faith, not having received the promises, but having seen them afar off, and were persuaded of them, and embraced them, and confessed that they were strangers and pilgrims on the earth. For they that say such things declare plainly that they seek a country....But now they desire a better country, that is, an heavenly: wherefore God is not ashamed to be called their God: for he hath prepared for them a city" (He.11:8-10, 13-14, 16).

"But ye are come unto mount Sion, and unto the city of the living God, the heavenly Jerusalem, and to an innumerable company of angels" (He.12:22).

"For here have we no continuing city, but we seek one to come" (He.13:14).

"But the day of the Lord will come as a thief in the night; in the which the heavens shall pass away with a great noise, and the elements shall melt with fervent heat, the earth also and the works that are therein shall be burned up. Seeing then that all these things shall be dissolved, what manner of persons ought ye to be in all holy conversation and godliness, looking for and hasting unto the coming of the day of God, wherein the heavens being on fire shall be dissolved, and the elements shall melt with fervent heat? Nevertheless we, according to his promise, look for new heavens and a new earth, wherein dwelleth righteousness" (2 Pe.3:10-13).

"And I saw a new heaven and a new earth: for the first heaven and the first earth were passed away" (Re.21:1).

OUTLINE BIBLE RESOURCES

This material, like similar works, has come from imperfect man and is thus susceptible to human error. We are nevertheless grateful to God for both calling us and empowering us through His Holy Spirit to undertake this task. Because of His goodness and grace, *The Preacher's Outline & Sermon Bible*® New Testament and the Old Testament volumes are now complete.

The Minister's Personal Handbook, The Believer's Personal Handbook, and other helpful **Outline Bible Resources** are available in printed form as well as releasing electronically on various software programs.

God has given the strength and stamina to bring us this far. Our confidence is that as we keep our eyes on Him and remain grounded in the undeniable truths of the Word, we will continue to produce other helpful Outline Bible Resources for God's dear servants to use in their Bible Study and discipleship.

We offer this material, first, to Him in whose name we labor and serve and for whose glory it has been produced and, second, to everyone everywhere who studies, preaches, and teaches the Word.

Our daily prayer is that each volume will lead thousands, millions, yes even billions, into a better understanding of the Holy Scriptures and a fuller knowledge of Jesus Christ the Incarnate Word, of whom the Scriptures so faithfully testify.

You will be pleased to know that Leadership Ministries Worldwide partners with Christian organizations, printers, and mission groups around the world to make Outline Bible Resources available and affordable in many countries and foreign languages. It is our goal that *every* leader around the world, both clergy and lay, will be able to understand God's Holy Word and present God's message with more clarity, authority, and understanding—all beyond his or her own power.

LEADERSHIP MINISTRIES WORLDWIDE

1928 Central Avenue • Chattanooga, TN 37408
(423) 855-2181 FAX (423) 855-8616
info@lmw.org
www.lmw.org – FREE download materials

6/16

- **THE PREACHER'S OUTLINE & SERMON BIBLE®** (POSB) • **KJV – NIV**

NEW TESTAMENT

Matthew 1 (chapters 1–15)	1 & 2 Corinthians
Matthew 2 (chapters 16–28)	Galatians, Ephesians, Philippians, Colossians
Mark	1 & 2 Thessalonians, 1 & 2 Timothy, Titus, Philemon
Luke	Hebrews, James
John	1 & 2 Peter, 1, 2, & 3 John, Jude
Acts	Revelation
Romans	Master Outline & Subject Index

OLD TESTAMENT

Genesis 1 (chapters 1–11)	1 Kings	Isaiah 1 (chapters 1-35)
Genesis 2 (chapters 12–50)	2 Kings	Isaiah 2 (chapters 36-66)
Exodus 1 (chapters 1–18)	1 Chronicles	Jeremiah 1 (chapters 1-29)
Exodus 2 (chapters 19–40)	2 Chronicles	Jeremiah 2 (chapters 30-52),
Leviticus	Ezra, Nehemiah, Esther	Lamentations
Numbers	Job	Ezekiel
Deuteronomy	Psalms 1 (chapters 1-41)	Daniel, Hosea
Joshua	Psalms 2 (chapters 42-106)	Joel, Amos, Obadiah, Jonah,
Judges, Ruth	Psalms 3 (chapters 107-150)	Micah, Nahum
1 Samuel	Proverbs	Habakkuk, Zephaniah, Haggai,
2 Samuel	Ecclesiastes, Song of Solomon	Zechariah, Malachi

Print versions of all Outline Bible Resources are available in various forms.

- **The Preacher's Outline & Sermon Bible New Testament — 3 Vol. Hardcover • KJV – NIV**
- ***What the Bible Says to the Believer* — The Believer's Personal Handbook**
  11 Chs. – Over 500 Subjects, 300 Promises, & 400 Verses Expounded - Italian Imitation Leather or Paperback
- ***What the Bible Says to the Minister* — The Minister's Personal Handbook**
  12 Chs. - 127 Subjects - 400 Verses Expounded - Italian Imitation Leather or Paperback
- **Practical Word Studies In the New Testament — 2 Vol. Hardcover Set**
- **The Teacher's Outline & Study Bible™ - Various New Testament Books**
  Complete 30 - 45 minute lessons – with illustrations and discussion questions
- **Practical Illustrations — Companion to the POSB**
  Arranged by topic and Scripture reference
- **What the Bible Says About Series – Various Subjects**
- **OBR on various digital platforms**
  See current digital providers on our website at www.outlinebible.org
- **Non-English Translations of various books**

  See our website for more information or contact our office

— Contact LMW for quantity orders and information —

LEADERSHIP MINISTRIES WORLDWIDE or Your Local Christian Bookstore
1928 Central Avenue • Chattanooga, TN 37408
(423) 855-2181 (9am – 5pm Eastern) • FAX (423) 855-8616
E-mail - info@lmw.org • Order online at www.lmw.org

PURPOSE STATEMENT

Leadership Ministries Worldwide

exists to equip ministers, teachers, and laymen in their understanding, preaching, and teaching of God's Word by publishing and distributing worldwide *The Preacher's Outline & Sermon Bible*® and related **Outline Bible Resources;** to reach & disciple men, women, boys and girls for Jesus Christ.

MISSION STATEMENT

1. To make the Bible so understandable – its truth so clear and plain – that men and women everywhere, whether teacher or student, preacher or hearer, can grasp its message and receive Jesus Christ as Savior, and…

2. To place the Bible in the hands of all who will preach and teach God's Holy Word, verse by verse, precept by precept, regardless of the individual's ability to purchase it.

The **Outline Bible Resources** have been given to LMW for printing and distribution worldwide at/below cost, by those who remain anonymous. One fact, however, is as true today as it was in the time of Christ:

THE GOSPEL IS FREE, BUT THE COST OF TAKING IT IS NOT

LMW depends on the generous gifts of believers with a heart for Him and a love for the lost. They help pay for the printing, translating, and distributing of **Outline Bible Resources** into the hands of God's servants worldwide, who will present the Gospel message with clarity, authority, and understanding beyond their own.

LMW was incorporated in the state of Tennessee in July 1992 and received IRS 501 (c)(3) non-profit status in March 1994. LMW is an international, nondenominational mission organization. All proceeds from USA sales, along with donations from donor partners, go directly to underwrite translation and distribution projects of **Outline Bible Resources** to preachers, church and lay leaders, and Bible students around the world.

CPSIA information can be obtained
at www.ICGtesting.com
Printed in the USA
LVHW051423030420
652136LV00017B/1391